EASTERN GREAT LAKES LIGHTHOUSES

BY BRUCE ROBERTS *and* RAY JONES

New England Lighthouses
Bay of Fundy to Long Island Sound

Mid-Atlantic Lighthouses
Hudson River to Chesapeake Bay

Southeastern Lighthouses
Outer Banks to Cape Florida

Gulf Coast Lighthouses
Florida Keys to the Rio Grande

California Lighthouses
Point St. George to the Gulf of Santa Catalina

Pacific Northwest Lighthouses
Oregon, Washington, Alaska, and British Columbia

Western Great Lakes Lighthouses
Michigan and Superior

Eastern Great Lakes Lighthouses
Ontario, Erie, and Huron

LIGHTHOUSES SERIES

THE LIFE AND HISTORY OF AMERICA'S WATERWAYS

EASTERN
Great Lakes
LIGHTHOUSES

ONTARIO, ERIE, *and* HURON

PHOTOGRAPHS *by* BRUCE ROBERTS
TEXT *by* RAY JONES

CHELSEA HOUSE PUBLISHERS

Philadelphia

Although a Fresnel lens may look like a single piece of molded glass, it consists of many separate, hand-polished prisms fitted into a metal frame. The prisms gather light, focusing it into a concentrated beam. Invented by French physicist Augustin Fresnel in 1822 and introduced in America some decades later, the chandelierlike Fresnel lenses made lighthouse beacons much more powerful and reliable. Manufactured in Paris and shipped across the Atlantic in pieces, a Fresnel would be painstakingly reassembled inside the lighthouse lantern room. Fresnels came in a variety of sizes, or "orders," ranging from sixth-order (about seventeen inches high and a foot wide) to first-order (as much as ten feet high and six feet wide). Most Fresnels used on the Great Lakes were third-, fourth-, or fifth-order lenses. Many, though certainly not all, of the old Fresnels have been replaced by automated, airport-style beacons. But this third-order Fresnel still shines from the lantern room of the Point Gratiot Lighthouse in Dunkirk, New York.

First Chelsea House hardback edition published 2000.

All photographs, unless otherwise credited, are by Bruce Roberts.
Editorial research by Cheryl Shelton-Roberts
Cover and text design by Nancy Freeborn

Library of Congress Cataloging-in-Publication Data
Roberts, Bruce, 1930–
    Eastern Great Lakes lighthouses : Ontario, Erie, and Huron / photos by Bruce Roberts ; text by Ray Jones.
      p. cm — (The lighthouse series)Originally published: Old Saybrook, CT : Globe Pequot Press, 1996.
    Includes bibliographical references and index.
    Summary: Provides historical background and descriptive information on some of the most significant lighthouses on Lakes Ontario, Erie, and Huron.
    ISBN 0-7910-5487-X
    1. Lighthouses—Great Lakes—History. [1. Lighthouses—Ontario, Lake (N.Y. and Ont.)—History.
    2. Lighthouses—Erie, Lake—History. 3. Lighthouses—Huron, Lake (Mich. and Ont.)—History.] I. Jones,
    Ray, 1948- . II. Title. III. Series: Lighthouse series (Philadelphia, Pa.)
VK1023.3.R627 1999
387.1'55'0977—dc21   99-15007
                                                CIP

Front-cover photograph: Marblehead Light, Bay Point, Ohio
Back-cover photograph: Cove Island Light, Lake Huron, Canada

Printed in Malaysia   **1 2 3 4 5 6 7 8 9 10**

To MARION *and* WES ROBERTS

Tibbetts Point Lighthouse graces the horizon of a New York sunset.

ACKNOWLEDGMENTS

When my wife, Cheryl, and I started out photographing lighthouses on the Great Lakes, we had no idea how many people would help us along the way. Jeanne and George Couglar, caretakers at Tibbetts Point Light at Cape Vincent, New York, gave us the run of the place. Also, thanks go to Shirley Hamblen, founder and past president of the Tibbetts Point Lighthouse Historical Society. Dick and Barb Lawson at Point Gratiot Lighthouse in Dunkirk, New York, came back at night so I could get the wonderful shot of the Fresnel lens on page iv ; Ken Black of the Shore Museum in Rockland, Maine, sent us photocopies of the Old Lighthouse Service bulletins. At Thirty Mile Lighthouse in New York, Thomas Harris loaned us his scrapbook. Wayne Wheeler and Marie Shaft at the United States Lighthouse Society shared information from the files in San Francisco.

Back in Washington, D.C., Dr. Robert M. Browning, historian of the United States Coast Guard, was there with a helping hand. Candace Clifford of the National Park Service Maritime Initiative compiled facts on American lighthouses. James Cassedy of the National Archives, Suitland Reference Division, found our lost notes and request for photocopies. James W. Claflin of Kenrick A. Claflin & Son, dealers in nautical antiques in Northborough, Massachusetts, took in earnest our needs and requests for early lighthouse records.

A special thanks to David Kramer of Lorain, Ohio, who supplied not only the information about the lighthouse there but also the wonderful photograph that shows the light leaning just a bit—the leaning lighthouse of Lorain, as I love to call it. In Canada, Helen Van Everey of Meldrum Bay, Ontario, supplied us with an excellent photo of the Mississagi Lighthouse on Manitoulin Island.

And thanks to my wife, Cheryl, for putting up with long drives and late hours, for keeping notes that I would have lost, for carrying camera equipment up and down countless steps to lighthouses, and for smiles at the end of exhausting days.

—*Bruce Roberts*

Special thanks to Arthur Layton for his time and expertise in helping obtain information for the expansive area covered by this book.

—*Ray Jones*

CONTENTS

INTRODUCTION
page 1

Chapter One
LIGHTS OF THE GATEWAY LAKE
Ontario
page 5

Chapter Two
LIGHTS OF THE WARRIOR LAKE
Erie
page 23

Chapter Three
LIGHTS OF THE THUNDER LAKE
Huron
page 43

Chapter Four
LIGHTS OF THE IMPERIAL COAST
The Canadian Shores
page 59

BIBLIOGRAPHY
page 83

LIGHTHOUSES INDEX
page 84

FOR FURTHER INFORMATION ON LIGHTHOUSES
page 85

PHOTO INFORMATION
page 87

Shaped something like the potbellied stove on the left, a delicate Fresnel lens (probably fourth-order) takes center stage in this turn-of-the-century Lighthouse Service Depot in Buffalo. Similar workshops throughout the Great Lakes region kept lighthouse lenses and equipment in top condition. (Courtesy National Archives)

INTRODUCTION

Among the thousands of vessels that have been lost on the Great Lakes was the very first European-style trading ship to sail the lakes' wide, open waters. In 1679 the French explorer Sieur de La Salle and a party of fur traders built a fifty-ton sailing ship, pushing it off into Lake Erie from a rough-hewn shipyard near where the city of Buffalo, New York, now stands. This was no crude, overbuilt canoe. Christened the *Griffin*, it was more than sixty feet long and had five cannon arrayed below the deck. La Salle and his fellow adventurers intended to make themselves rich by filling the *Griffin*'s holds with muskrat and beaver pelts gathered by French trappers.

The *Griffin* proved a worthy ship, weathering more than one fierce storm on the outbound leg of its maiden voyage to the far reaches of the Great Lakes. Eventually, La Salle disembarked to continue his explorations (and discover the upper Mississippi River). As he watched the *Griffin* sail away eastward, La Salle was confident that the ship and her treasured cargo of furs would safely reach their destination. But neither the *Griffin* nor her crew was ever heard from again. Probably, like so many other unlucky ships that came after, she was smashed by a sudden, sharp autumn gale. Some believe that her rotting ribs lie near the Mississagi Straits Lighthouse on Lake Huron. If the lighthouse had been there to guide the *Griffin* when it sailed into the straits more than 300 years ago, perhaps commercial shipping on the Great Lakes would not have gotten off to such an unfortunate and ominous beginning.

AMERICA'S INLAND SEAS

Ontario. Erie. Huron. Michigan. Superior. These are no ordinary lakes. First consider their size. A journey from Cleveland, Ohio, on the southern shore of Lake Erie, to Duluth, Minnesota, on the western reaches of Lake Superior, will cover more than 700 miles—and on this trip the traveler would not traverse the 307-mile length of Lake Michigan or the 193-mile length of Lake Ontario.

The lakes are so large that they are easily recognized from space. They have been seen and identified by astronauts standing on the moon.

Taken together, the Great Lakes comprise by far the largest body of freshwater on the planet. They form what is quite literally an inland freshwater sea. As such, they invite comparison to the Earth's other great seas: the Red, the Black, the Baltic, the North, the Caspian, the Aral (actually much smaller than Lake Superior), and others. But the most interesting and instructive comparison to be made is with the world's most famous sea, the Mediterranean.

Born in a desert, the Mediterranean was once an enormous, sandy basin with a mostly dry, sun-scorched floor. When Spain parted from the African continent several million years ago, the Atlantic poured through the Strait of Gibraltar, also known as the "Gates of Hercules," and turned the desert into a sea. The Mediterranean retains some of the qualities of a sunny desert even today. It evaporates more water than it receives from its rivers. Thus, should the movements of the continents ever close the strait, the Mediterranean would eventually dry up and become once more a parched basin. In contrast, if some geological upheaval were suddenly to reverse the flow of the St. Lawrence River (and the upper Mississippi), the watery abundance of the Great Lakes would inundate the entire Midwest.

The lakes were the product not of a desert environment, however, but of a frozen one. Four times during the last million years, heavy blankets of ice reached southward across the North American continent. After each advance the ice retreated, leaving behind enormous lakes. The last of these ice ages, known to scientists as the Wisconsin Advance, ended about 10,000 years ago—in geological time, a blink of an eye. Relative to the age of the Earth, which is measured in billions of years, the lakes that we see today are very young indeed. And when their waters are torn by the storms that come whistling out of the center of the continent, they show their youthful temper.

Although they are unruly children by comparison, the lakes have more than a little in common with the much older and larger Mediterranean Sea. Both these mostly enclosed bodies of water are products of a geological revolution, and both have nurtured a revolution. The trade made possible by the readily navigable waters of the Mediterranean formed the economic basis of Greek culture, the Roman Empire—indeed, of all Western civilization. Many centuries later the freighters scurrying back and forth through the Great Lakes would fuel another economic miracle: the American Industrial Renaissance. These changes, however—though most would call them beneficial to humanity—came at a heavy price.

As Ulysses and countless sailors of later eras have discovered, those who sail the Earth's salt- or freshwater seas for commerce or adventure may get far more than they bargained for. The floor of the Mediterranean is a graveyard littered with the hulks of rotting ships. Similarly, the Great Lakes serve as a vast tomb for wrecked ships and their hapless crews. At least 6,000 large vessels have found their final resting place at the bottom of the five lakes.

The Great Lakes have always presented a special challenge for sailors. Because they are located near the center of one of the Earth's largest land masses, the weather patterns that sweep across the lakes are quite different from—and often more violent than—those encountered on the open ocean. North America receives heavier snows than any other continent, so the lakes are the snowiest navigable bodies of water on the planet.

But potentially blinding snow squalls are only one of the lake sailor's many concerns. Storms driven by the sharp temperature differences over land and over water can strike swiftly and with extraordinary intensity. Skies may clear again in a matter of minutes, or the heavy weather may go on for days. Since freshwater is lighter than salt water, wind-driven waves that batter the sides of ships tend to mount higher. The lakes' narrow widths and even narrower channels leave ships little room to maneuver. And there are countless ship-killing shoals and low, almost invisible headlands waiting to devour any vessel and crew that stray too far off course.

The lakes are so unpredictable and, at times, so dangerous that regular commercial shipping would be impossible without an extensive, well-planned network of navigational aides. Today the U.S. and Canadian Coast Guards help guide ships through the lakes with an increasing array of high-tech direction-finding equipment, radio beacons, and radar. Thousands of buoys and channel lights have made well-marked highways of the lakes.

One might almost think that lake navigators should stow their charts and compasses and buy road maps. But not so. Most of the time—and always in a storm—lake sailors are on their own. They must rely on their eyes and their own good judgment to help them get around safely from place to place. And on a dark night or in a gale, when captains or pilots are seen with binoculars in hand, they are most likely looking for the beacon of a lighthouse.

Lighthouses became the subject of one of the very first acts of the new Congress in 1789, when responsibility for construction and operation of coastal lights was placed in the hands of the Treasury Department. Eight years earlier, the British had placed a beacon in the tower at Fort Niagara (above), although both tower and light were gone by 1806. Alexander Hamilton, whose face looks out at us from the $100 bill, became the first head of the Lighthouse Service. Among Hamilton's successors was Stephen Pleasonton, a Treasury auditor who presided over the service like an Oriental satrap for nearly half a century. Pleasonton's tight-fisted stodginess delayed introduction of the advanced Fresnel lens for decades. A Lighthouse Board comprising engineers and maritime professionals replaced Pleasonton in 1852 and made rapid improvements in America's growing list of navigational lights. The board promoted widespread use of the powerful French-made Fresnels.

From 1910 until 1939 the service was run by a separate government Bureau of Lighthouses. Then, just before World War II, responsibility for lighthouses was placed entirely in the hands of the U.S. Coast Guard. Since then many lighthouses have been discontinued, and all but one (the Boston Harbor Lighthouse) have been automated. Sadly, the lighthouse keeper is now a nearly extinct professional species in the United States.

LIGHTING *the* WAY

For as long as ships have sailed the seas, sailors nearing land have counted on shore lights to help them determine their positions, avoid dangerous obstacles, and find safe harbor. The earliest maritime peoples banked fires on hillsides to bring their ships home from the sea. Occasionally, port cities and towns lacking suitable high ground for this purpose erected towers and placed a lamp or built a small fire at the top.

No one can say where the world's first true lighthouse was located, but the first that we know of served the Greco–Egyptian city of Alexandria. Soaring 450 feet into the sunny Mediterranean skies, it was also history's tallest lighthouse and the one with the longest service record. Built about 280 B.C. on an island called Pharos, inside Alexandria's bustling harbor, it stood for more than a thousand years before being toppled by an earthquake near the end of the first millennium A.D.

At night keepers lit a bright fire at the top of the huge tower to guide Phoenicians, Greeks, Carthaginians, Romans, and other mariners from all over the known world to this fabled and prosperous city. Most came to load up their ships with grain from the Nile Delta. The rich soil of the delta was so wondrously productive that its grains made possible the Roman Empire and fed soldiers and city dwellers all around the Mediterranean Basin. But the grain would never have reached market without the ships that carried it and the lighthouse that guided their captains to port.

Like the Mediterranean of Roman times, North America's inland seas are a heavily traveled commercial thoroughfare. Great Lakes freighters carry an endless variety of raw materials and finished products—iron ore to steel mills, metal parts to auto-assembly plants, oil and chemicals to refineries, grain from the prodigious farms of the Midwest to hungry peoples all over the world. The Great Lakes have been a key driving force in the American economy, and the long lake freighters and their brave crews have fueled that engine. But the prosperity brought by commerce has come at a high price: thousands of ships sunk and thousands of sailors drowned.

Yet the cost in vessels and lives would have been even higher if not for the lighthouses that ring each of the lakes. For more than a century, lake sailors have been guided by a linked chain of navigational lights extending for more than a thousand miles, from the St. Lawrence River to Duluth. Many of the lights, such as the Charlotte-Genesee light in Rochester, New York, or the Gibraltar Point Light in Toronto, Ontario, have shined out over the lake waters since the United States and Canada were very young nations. Most lake lighthouses are at least a century old, and all have played an essential role in the economic development and history of the United States and Canada.

Through dramatic photographs and narrative, this book tells the story of the most historically significant and scenic lighthouses on Lakes Ontario, Erie, and Huron. (Be sure to read about the lights on Lakes Michigan and Superior in our book *Western Great Lakes Lighthouses,* published by The Globe Pequot Press.) Travel information is included for those who wish to discover these architectural and historic treasures for themselves. Join us now as we follow a trail of lighthouses leading deep into the heart of a continent.

CHAPTER ONE

Lights of
THE GATEWAY LAKE
ONTARIO

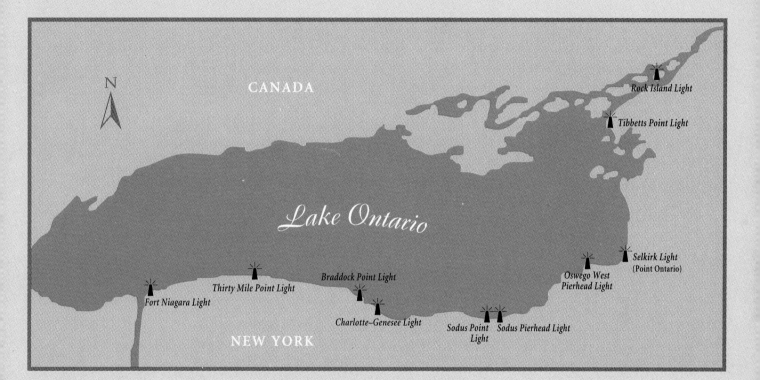

CANADA

Rock Island Light

Tibbetts Point Light

Lake Ontario

Selkirk Light
(Point Ontario)

Oswego West
Pierhead Light

Thirty Mile Point Light

Braddock Point Light

Fort Niagara Light

Charlotte–Genesee Light

Sodus Point
Light

Sodus Pierhead Light

NEW YORK

A freshwater inland sea, Lake Ontario attracts plenty of gulls—not to mention ships, which need navigational lights to guide them safely to port. Just off New York's Sodus Point, the lighthouse above stands at the end of a lengthy pier, an arrangement characteristic of many Great Lakes lighthouses.

*L*ighthouses are among the most prominent and recognizable manmade structures on the planet. Precisely because of their status as navigational markers, they are closely identified with certain geographic or natural features. For instance, it is difficult to think of Ohio's Marblehead Peninsula as separate from the Marblehead Lighthouse or Ontario's Gibraltar Point as separate from the Gibraltar Point Lighthouse. Lighthouse towers seem almost the products of nature, as if they had been carved from native stone and left behind by the retreating glaciers of the last ice age. Of course, the Great Lakes themselves, which provide the reason for most of America's inland lighthouses, were in fact created by this chiseling action of ice and water on stone.

Each of the Earth's continents has at least one natural feature that stands out in our minds as a symbol for all its diverse lands and peoples. For Africa, that feature is probably the Nile; for Asia, Mount Everest; for Australia, Ayers Rock; for South America, the Amazon; for Europe, the Alps or perhaps the Greek Isles. But since most of us reading this book live in North America and have differing regional loyalties, the selection of such a symbol for this continent may seem a little more difficult. For instance, some might put forward the Mississippi River, while others may suggest Mount McKinley, the Colorado Rockies, or the California redwoods. Upon reflection, however, the available choices can easily be reduced to one.

A few miles from the city of Buffalo, New York, is a natural phenomenon so majestic and so powerful that every year it strikes millions of people speechless with awe. Tourists flock to see it from every state in the Union, every Canadian province, and, literally, every nation on Earth. Children the world over have heard of this place and, no doubt, dreamed of traveling to America to enjoy it for themselves. The phenomenon in question is, of course, Niagara Falls.

Actually a pair of falls, the American and Horseshoe, one on either side of the U.S.–Canadian border, they form what is arguably the world's most popular and most visited natural wonder. And why not? Fed by the overflow from four of the Earth's largest lakes, the falls are very impressive indeed. More than 40 million gallons of water plunge over them every minute. This unforgettable display of nature's raw power has inspired poets, politicians, and countless ordinary people, not to mention generations of young couples who have flocked to the falls to celebrate, and consummate, their marriages.

MARRIAGE *of* WATERS

Why do the Niagara Falls exert such a pull on us? Maybe it is because they help us understand our place in the natural scheme of things. Certainly, the falls are a key to understanding the Great Lakes and the leviathan geological forces that created them. Hundreds of millions of years ago, this region was covered by a warm, shallow sea teeming with life. Along the margins of the sea, colonies of tiny, shelled creatures piling one atop the other over millions of years built up an immense barrier reef. Eventually, the land was uplifted, the seas drained, and the ancient reef compacted into tough limestone.

Several times during the past million years, great sheets of ice up, to two miles thick, have pushed across the northern half of the continent. Like frozen bulldozers with blades a thousand miles wide, they scooped out basins. When the ice melted it filled the basins with water, forming lakes. But the stubborn limestone had resisted the ice and remained behind as a natural dike at the eastern end of Lake Erie. Today the waters of Erie, Huron, Michigan, and Superior spill over the dike, dropping several hundred feet in just a few miles on the way to Lake Ontario. The most dramatic descent is, of course, at Niagara, where the blue lake water plunges 184 feet over American Falls and 176 feet over Horseshoe Falls.

THE BEAVER CONNECTION

Among the very first Europeans to see the falls was Samuel de Champlain, father of New France and founder of the city of Quebec. Champlain pushed up the St. Lawrence River, explored Lake Ontario, and may have reached Niagara as early as 1604, several years before the English established their first colony in Virginia at Jamestown. No doubt the majesty of the falls impressed Champlain, but the French adventurer had much more to awe him besides: an entire pristine and unexplored new world. The Huron Indians told Champlain that beyond the falls lay several lakes even bigger than Ontario and a vast, wild region rich in furs and minerals. Initially, Champlain may have doubted their stories, but he and other astonished French explorers would soon learn that they were true. The falls were fed by an enormous system of swift-running rivers and huge lakes, reaching back a thousand miles or more into the very heartland of the North American continent. The French quickly saw the potential of all these interconnected waterways—they could be used as a convenient and highly profitable commercial highway.

It has been said that, more than any human adventurer, the humble beaver deserves credit for opening up the North American interior. Much prized by hatmakers and the fashion-conscious ladies and gentlemen of Europe, beaver pelts gave tough French trappers a cash incentive for exploring America. Following every river and stream all the way to its source, they loaded sturdy bark canoes with pelts and then paddled and portaged them eastward along at least part of what is known today as the St. Lawrence Seaway.

It may be that the French built signal fires or placed lanterns on poles to guide their canoe freighters to key portages, villages, and fur-trading centers. It was the British, however, who would build the first true lighthouse on the Great Lakes.

For more than 150 years, the British wrestled with the French for control of the lakes and the access they provided to the interior of the continent. This struggle reached its climax in 1759, during the French and Indian War, when an army of redcoats, under the command of General James Wolfe, appeared outside the city walls of Quebec. The Marquis de Montcalm rushed out from behind the walls at the head of a poorly trained force of irregulars to confront Wolfe and was promptly defeated. Although both commanders were killed, the battle ended in near total defeat for the French. Having captured Quebec, the city of Champlain, the British took possession of Canada and the strategic Great Lakes waterways. But complete British dominion over the lakes would be short-lived.

REVOLUTIONARY GHOST SHIP

Only fifteen years after their victory over the French, the British found themselves once more at war in America. This time the fight was against their own unruly colonists. During this Revolutionary War the British maintained a powerful navy on the Great Lakes. Among their most formidable lake warships was HMS *Ontario*. Launched during the late spring of 1780, she was at least eighty feet long and square-rigged like an oceangoing fighting ship. Armed with sixteen 6-pound cannon and six 4-pounders, she had more than enough firepower to crush any American vessel that might challenge her mastery of Lake Ontario. The weather and the lake itself, however, could not be fought with cannon shot and gunpowder. The *Ontario* was destined to lose its only battle—with one of the Great Lakes' notorious autumn storms.

Late in October 1780, the *Ontario* weighed anchor and set sail from Niagara, bound for Oswego, New York, with a load of British soldiers, military supplies, and an army payroll chest brimming with gold and silver coins. On Halloween a gale came whistling out of the west, and by the time it had blown itself out the following morning, the *Ontario* was gone. Vanishing along with it were four women, five children, several Indians, and more than seventy soldiers and seamen. As with the *Edmund Fitzgerald* and so many other disappearances on the Great Lakes, this one remains a mystery to this day. Poignantly, settlers found dozens of British Army caps bobbing in the waves along the south shore of the lake; but there were no other clues to the fate of the ship or its passengers, crew, and cargo. Treasure hunters, interested in valuable relics—not to mention the payroll chest—have searched endlessly for the wreck. Most believe the *Ontario* met its end near Thirty Mile Point. The discovery in 1954 of a very old anchor not far from the point lends weight to this opinion, but the ship itself has never been found.

Ironically, countless sailors may owe their lives indirectly to the sinking of the *Ontario*. The loss of this fine ship alerted British authorities to the need for better navigation markers on the Great Lakes. In 1781, the year after the *Ontario* disaster, they placed a light, fueled by whale oil, on the roof of Fort Niagara, at the mouth of the Niagara River. The French had built the old stone fortress in 1726 to help protect fur traders portaging their pelts from the upper lakes. The British had taken control of the fort after the French and Indian War. The fort and its light, the first established on the Great Lakes, became the property of the United States following the Revolutionary War.

For more than fifty-seven years, the Braddock Point Lighthouse marked the western approaches to the city of Rochester, New York. Focused by a 3.5-order lens, its 20,000-candlepower light was among the brightest on the Great Lakes. Ships' captains reported seeing the light from more than eighteen miles out on Lake Ontario.

The extraordinary tower was also one of the lake's most distinctive daymarks. Built during the mid-1890s, at the height of the Victorian era, it featured a decorative gallery and peaked roof suggestive of the elaborate helmet of a European calvary officer.

Unfortunately, the old lighthouse weathered one too many of Lake Ontario's prodigious storms. By 1954 the structure had suffered damage so extensive the the building itself became a safety hazard. The Coast Guard had no choice but to extinguish the light and pull down the top two thirds of the tower, to keep it from falling under its own weight. Today the Braddock Point Lighthouse, with its squat, truncated tower, is a private residence closed to the public. (Courtesy National Archives)

ROCK ISLAND LIGHT

Rock Island, New York – 1847 and 1882

To reach the Great Lakes from the Atlantic Ocean, ships must push several hundred miles up the ever-narrowing St. Lawrence River. Toward the end of this river journey are the Thousand Islands, which guard the approaches to Lake Ontario. Six lighthouses were built along the river and among the islands to guide ships and warn them of obstacles. One of the best preserved of these is the Rock Island Lighthouse, established in 1847 and rebuilt in 1882.

The Rock Island Lighthouse has its feet in the river.

Built just off the island on a concrete foundation, the forty-foot, conical limestone tower is connected to land by a stone walkway. The lantern once held a sixth-order Fresnel lens, but following World War II, the station was deactivated and the old lens removed. At one time the lamps were powered by a gasoline generator located in a separate structure near the dwelling. Active for almost a century, the light serves tens of thousands of vessels steaming along the St. Lawrence, going to and from the Great Lakes.

The mighty St. Lawrence River surrounds the Rock Island Light Station. (Courtesy U.S. Coast Guard)

HOW TO GET THERE:

Rock Island is accessible only from the water, and while no public transportation to the island is available, private boats may stop here. The lighthouse is usually open to the public from 8:00 A.M. to 4:30 P.M. during the summer months, but it is best to make sure by calling ahead. For information call (315) 654–2522. The lighthouse can also be seen from Thousand Island Park, on Wellesley Island, and from the community of Fisher's Landing, off Route 12 at Route 180, just a few miles southwest of the Thousand Island Bridge. For information on events and facilities in the Thousand Islands region, write the Thousand Islands International Council, Box 400, Alexandria Bay, New York 13607, or call (800) 8–ISLAND.

TIBBETTS POINT LIGHT

Cape Vincent, New York – 1827 and 1854

Lighthouses are nearly always strategically located, but that is especially true of Tibbetts Point Lighthouse in Cape Vincent, New York. Its light marks the entrance to the St. Lawrence River and the beginning of the last leg of any journey from the Great Lakes to the Atlantic. Recognizing the importance of the place to commercial shipping, the government placed a light station here in 1827. The stone tower stood fifty-nine feet high and employed a whale-oil lamp and reflector lighting system.

The light tower that can be seen at Cape Vincent today replaced the earlier lighthouse in 1854. Its sixty-

Countless vessels sailing from Lake Ontario to the Atlantic Ocean have passed by the sixty-nine-foot tower of Tibbetts Point Lighthouse. Since 1854 the stucco structure has stood the test of wind, weather, and time.

nine-foot stucco tower was given a fourth-order Fresnel lens lighted by a fifty-candlepower oil lamp. A steam-powered fog signal began operation in 1896. The station was automated by the Coast Guard in 1981.

Cape Vincent has spectacular sunsets, and the lighthouse grounds offer an excellent place to view and photograph them. Nearby are several historic islands, including Wolfe Island, named for the British general who captured Quebec, and Carleton Island, a frequent gathering place for large Mohawk war parties.

The sun drops into Lake Ontario behind the tower of Tibbetts Point Lighthouse. Located where Ontario's waters flow into the St. Lawrence River, the lighthouse marks the eastern limits of the Great Lakes region. Not surprisingly, this is an excellent site for early evening photography.

HOW TO GET THERE:

To reach the lighthouse from Cape Vincent and New York Highway 12E, follow Lighthouse Road for 2½ miles to the cape. The grounds are open daily for walking, picnicking, and photography. The keeper's house now serves as an American Youth Hostel, open from May 15 to October 15. For hostel reservations call (315) 654–3450. This is a gorgeous place for sunset photographs.

SELKIRK (PORT ONTARIO) LIGHT

Selkirk (Pulaski), New York – 1838

Although its beacon served lake sailors for little more than twenty years, the Selkirk Lighthouse is one of the more fascinating and historic buildings on the Great Lakes. Built in 1838, it was taken out of service in 1859, when the local fishing and shipbuilding industries began to fade. Fortunately, the old lighthouse has survived. Its gabled fieldstone dwelling and old-style lantern are of considerable architectural and historical interest.

The first settlers came to Port Ontario to harvest the Atlantic salmon that came here in prodigious numbers to spawn. The fishermen were followed by sailors and shipbuilders, who built homes beside the lake and along the banks of the appropriately named Salmon River. In one way or another, most of the men in the area relied for their living on Lake Ontario. With its dangerous, unpredictable weather, the lake was a fickle and sometimes death-dealing friend. That is why, according to legend, houses hereabouts have an unusually large number of windows, for the wives of fishermen and sailors kept a constant eye on the lake for some sign of their menfolk.

The Selkirk Lighthouse also has its share of windows. Built for $3,000 by local contractors with stone quarried nearby, the old dwelling is one of a kind. The small lantern room projecting through the roof is also highly unusual. It is of an early type in use before Fresnel lenses became common (about the middle of the nineteenth century). Originally, the lantern held a fourteen-inch parabolic reflector and eight mineral-oil lamps. The light could be seen from about fourteen miles out on the lake. Shortly before the lighthouse was discontinued, the outdated reflector system was replaced by a sixth-order Fresnel lens.

When the Salmon River began to silt up and ship traffic dropped off, the government saw little need for a light here. The building was eventually sold for use as a private residence and then as a hotel. Although its lantern was dark for more than 130 years, the old lighthouse is now back in operation. In 1989 the owners received permission from the Coast Guard to place an automated light in the lantern. The light is designated a Class 11 navigational aid.

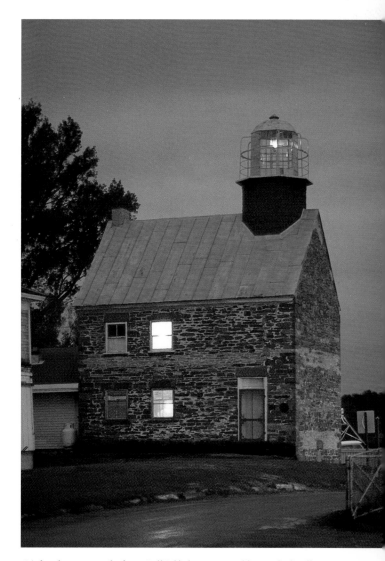

Light glows warmly from Selkirk's lantern and keeper's dwelling, now a rustic hostelry frequented by salmon fishermen.

HOW TO GET THERE:

The lighthouse is privately owned and not open to the public. It can, however, be seen from the road. Take Route 3, which parallels the lakeshore a few miles west of I–81, to Port Ontario, and turn onto Lake Road. The lighthouse stands at the end of the road, at the mouth of the Salmon River. The old stone lighthouse is being restored by the owners, who rent it for overnight accommodation. Here's a wonderful chance to spend the night in a real lighthouse. For information call (315) 298–6688. This area is very popular with fishermen, who flock here when the salmon are running.

OSWEGO WEST PIERHEAD LIGHT

Oswego, New York – 1822, 1836, and 1934

Over the course of one and three-quarters centuries, at least three different lighthouses have served the port city of Oswego, guiding vessels in and out of its bustling harbor. The first, a simple stone tower and keeper's dwelling built in 1822, stood at Fort Ontario on the east bank of the Oswego River.

As shipping on Lake Ontario increased and Oswego grew into an important commercial center, the need for a better, more powerful light became apparent. In 1836 a fine new lighthouse was built, at the end of a long pier on the west side of the harbor. An octagonal gray tower with attached oil room, it boasted a third-order Fresnel lens displaying a fixed white light that could be seen from fifteen miles out on the lake.

Tended by several generations of keepers, the light burned for almost a century. The hearts of Ontario's sailors and Oswego's old-timers were saddened when the wrecking crews pulled down the old tower in 1930.

The government had no intention of leaving Oswego's harbor unmarked for long, however, and plans were already in the making for a third lighthouse. By 1934 it was in service. Consisting of a relatively short metal tower and a small attached dwelling, each with white walls and a red roof, the lighthouse stands on a concrete pier at the end of a long stone breakwater. Fitted with a rotating, fourth-order Fresnel lens, the lantern displays a flashing red light. Tinted window panels in the lantern give the light its characteristic color.

In 1942 several coastguardsmen drowned only a short distance from the lighthouse, during what was to have been a routine exchange of keepers. Not long afterward Coast Guard officials decided to automate the light.

Another historic Oswego attraction is Fort Ontario. Built as a frontier bastion by the British in 1755, during the French and Indian War, Fort Ontario fell to the forces of the Marquis de Montcalm in 1756. The French

destroyed the fort before retreating toward Quebec, where they themselves were eventually defeated. The British rebuilt the fortress, only to see it overrun by an army of American revolutionaries in 1778. During the War of 1812, the British returned to bombard and overwhelm the fort. The undermanned defenders had only six cannon, which were in such bad shape that they had been condemned. Fort Ontario also saw service in the Civil War and in World War II, when it was used as a refugee center.

HOW TO GET THERE:

Although the lighthouse itself is off limits to the public, it can be seen and enjoyed from several vantage points in Oswego. The best is probably Bretbeck Park. From Route 104, turn toward the lake onto West First Street. Turn left onto Van Buren and then right onto Lake Street. The park is just beyond Wright's Landing. While in the area you may want to visit Oswego's H. White Marine Museum or the locks of the historic Oswego Canal. Also nearby is Fort Ontario, where you can see the keeper's residence of the original Oswego Lighthouse.

SODUS POINT LIGHTHOUSE

Sodus Point, New York – 1825 and 1871

On June 19, 1813, the citizens of sleepy Sodus Point, New York, had an uncharacteristically noisy day. A British fleet had sailed across Lake Ontario and rudely awakened them with cannon fire. The British fleet landed troops, but the redcoats were stopped and eventually driven off by a hastily gathered force of militia. To raise the alarm, a local horseman rode, Paul Revere style, through the countryside to warn farms and villages that "the British are coming."

From 1825 until just after the turn of the century, Sodus Point Lighthouse offered mariners a different sort of warning: Its bright beacon announced clearly that land was near. Unexpected encounters with land are nearly always fatal to ships and all too often to their crews as well. Ship captains and residents in this area had petitioned Congress for a light to guide sailors safely into Sodus Bay. Eventually, they were rewarded by construction of a rough split-stone tower and dwelling.

Completed during the administration of President John Quincy Adams, these structures remained in use for more than forty years. Following the Civil War they fell into a sad state of disrepair, and the government replaced them with a forty-five-foot-high, square stone tower and and attached two-story dwelling. The light has been inactive since 1901, its job taken over by the nearby pier light.

Today the station structures are maintained by the Sodus Bay Historical Society. The dwelling now contains a delightful maritime museum. Visitors will want to see the 3.5-order Fresnel lens in the tower.

A grand survivor from an earlier time, the 1871 Sodus Point Lighthouse still stands at lake's edge. The light in the lantern room was extinguished in 1901, when the nearby pierhead lighthouse (shown on page 16) took over its duties. Today the venerable structure houses a maritime museum. Its tower offers visitors a fine view of Lake Ontario.

Looking something like a chess piece, the Sodus Point Pierhead Lighthouse still guides lake shipping. It stands at the end of a long concrete pier connecting it to the mainland. This makes the light easier to see from the water and, so, more useful to navigators.

HOW TO GET THERE:

To reach the Old Sodus Lighthouse, take Route 104, turn north on Route 14 into the village of Sodus Point, and then turn left onto Ontario Street (at the firehall). The lighthouse is open weekends from July to mid-October, but hours may vary. For information call (315) 483–4936. The tower can be climbed for a close-up look at the old Fresnel lens and a spectacular view of Sodus Bay and the lake beyond.

CHARLOTTE–GENESEE LIGHT

Rochester, New York – 1822

The Charlotte–Genesee Lighthouse was not built until well after the War of 1812. Had it been built earlier, it might have become the target of British cannon. During that war the British made repeated visits to the mouth of the Genesee River, blasting away at homes and businesses with heavy cannon. The redcoats never mounted a full-scale invasion of the place, however, perhaps because residents were always prepared to take up arms against them. Cannon balls fired by the British became prizes of local residents. Some were actually used for industrial purposes, such as crushing stone and grinding indigo.

Completed in 1822 at a cost of $3,301 and dropped from active service in 1881, Genesee Light is now the second-oldest lighthouse on the Great Lakes. The grand old lighthouse owes its existence in part to stu-dents of nearby Charlotte High School, who have made it their symbol. In 1965, when it was rumored that the lighthouse would be torn down, students at the school began a successful campaign to save the structure. Responding to student petitions and other public pressure, the government handed the lighthouse over to the Charlotte–Genesee Lighthouse Historical Society. The station has now been restored, and its museum is operated under a permanent charter from New York State. The Coast Guard contributed a Fresnel lens from its Cleveland (Ohio) station to the restoration effort.

More than 170 years ago, the forty-foot-high, octagonal limestone tower was erected on the edge of a bluff overlooking the mouth of the Genesee River and Lake Ontario beyond. David Denman, the station's first keeper, lived beside the tower in a rustic, two-room

The stone tower and brick dwelling at Charlotte–Genesee Lighthouse are two of the Great Lakes' most historic structures.

limestone cottage. Each night Denman trudged up the tower steps to light the ten Argand lamps that produced the light concentrated by a set of reflectors. These relatively inefficient reflectors were exchanged for a fourth-order Fresnel lens in 1852. The current two-and-a-half-story brick dwelling replaced the cottage in 1863.

As part of renovations at the Genesee light station, government crews built a pier, placing a second small lighthouse tower at the end. In 1853 an August nor'easter sent waves crashing over the pier, making it extremely difficult for keeper Samuel Phillips to reach the tower on the pier and fire up the lamp there. Former lighthouse keeper Cuyler Cook happened to be nearby with a boat and offered to row Phillips out to the tower. Cook paid for this generosity with his life. While Phillips was tending the lamp, the waves swamped Cook's boat and drowned him.

In 1884 lighthouse officials decided to move the primary light station's apparatus to the pier and abandon the original lighthouse. Luckily, the old octagonal tower survived a century of disuse and remains today as a reminder of an earlier, more romantic era. In 1974 the Genesee Lighthouse was placed on the National Register of Historic Places.

HOW TO GET THERE:

From the east, take the Seaway Trail (Lakeshore Boulevard), then follow Lake Avenue north to Holy Cross Church. From the west of Rochester, take Lake Ontario State Parkway to Lake Avenue. The lighthouse and its parking lot are located behind the church. The lighthouse complex is now leased to the Charlotte–Genesee Lighthouse Historical Society, which opens the tower and dwelling to the public on weekends. The grounds are open daily. Special tours are available by appointment. For information phone (716) 621–6179.

Visible through a narrow passageway, a spiral staircase leads upward to the lantern room atop the tower. As the date over the door confirms, the rough stone tower has stood since 1822.

THIRTY MILE POINT LIGHT

Somerset, New York – 1876

Located on a point of land thirty miles east of the mouth of the Niagara River, the square stone tower of Thirty Mile Point Lighthouse rises seventy-eight feet above the level of Lake Ontario. The scenic point on which the lighthouse stands is memorable, not only because it is a convenient mile marker but also because of the waves of history that have washed over this place.

In 1678 a twenty-ton sailing vessel under the command of the French explorer Sieur de La Salle was wrecked off the point. A century later, during the Revolutionary War, the British fighting ship HMS *Ontario* was believed to have gone down near Thirty Mile Point, with the loss of eighty-eight lives. A two-master armed with heavy cannon, the *Ontario* was carrying British troops for duty against continental forces in New York, as well as an Army payroll estimated at $15,000, when she foundered during a blizzard. Divers believe that the wreck lies on the lake bottom only a mile or two off Thirty Mile Point. In 1954 an anchor believed to be from the *Ontario* was recovered off the point and is displayed at the Fort Ontario Museum.

Some say that Golden Hill takes its name from the glittering Army payroll supposedly washed or brought ashore from the wreck. There have been no few unsuccessful attempts to dig up the treasure. A less dramatic explanation for the name, which has the support of local historians, is the profusion of goldenrod that once bloomed on an island off the point. The island has been eroded away, along with the dangerous sandbar that once lay off the point. Yet rumors of buried treasure at Golden Hill persist.

As long ago as 1834, a local farmer told his neighbors of being startled by a group of men who had rowed up Golden Hill Creek to dig up a chest from the creek bank. He said that they took the chest back to a waiting schooner. Similar stories were probably told during the Prohibition era of this century. It is said that smugglers often brought illicit shipments of liquor ashore here.

The Thirty Mile Point Lighthouse was built on Golden Hill in 1875, at a cost of $90,000. It remained in service until 1959, when the light was automated and transferred to a slender steel tower nearby. The gray square-cut stones of the original tower were shipped from Chaumont Bay near the St. Lawrence River and then hauled up the steep banks of Golden Hill.

A Fresnel lens manufactured in France was installed in the eight-foot-diameter lantern room. The handmade French lens concentrated the light produced by a kerosene flame to a strength of 600,000 candlepower. Sailors could see the light from up to eighteen miles away. In 1885 the kerosene flame was replaced with one of the earliest electric bulbs ever placed in a lighthouse. The light produced by the combination of the old Fresnel lens and Mr. Thomas Edison's newfangled invention became the strongest on Lake Ontario and the fourth strongest on the Great Lakes.

HOW TO GET THERE:

Today the Thirty Mile Point Lighthouse is one of the main attractions of Golden Hill State Park. The park offers campsites, picnic tables, a marina, and an engaging nature trail. Visitors can also take a self-guided tour of the lighthouse. From Route 18, drive north on Route 269 and then west on Lower Lake Road. For more information call Golden Hill State Park at (716) 795–3885.

FORT NIAGARA LIGHT

Youngstown, New York – 1781, 1823, and 1872

Located in Youngstown, New York, at the juncture of the Niagara River and Lake Ontario, Fort Niagara Lighthouse stands as a mute reminder of early struggles for economic and political dominance in North America. Now an automated light station, the stone building attached to the tower is leased from the Coast Guard by the Old Fort Niagara Association, which uses it as a museum and gift shop.

By the late seventeenth-century, the Niagara River and its portages around Niagara Falls, which connect Lake Ontario to Lake Erie and the upper Great Lakes, had become important to French fur traders as they ventured ever deeper into the continent's interior. In 1726 the French built Fort Niagara, which came to be known as the "French Castle." The French maintained a few sailing vessels on Lake Ontario, but canoes and

Recently retired, Fort Niagara Lighthouse has seen more than its share of history. Fur traders once gathered near here for the difficult overland portage to Lake Erie.

bateaux were the principal means of hauling freight and passengers. The French fort acted as a large daymark for these small vessels. They also followed the plume of vapor rising from Niagara Falls; it could be seen from up to forty miles out on the lake.

In 1759 the British captured Fort Niagara, one of the most valued prizes of the French and Indian War. Sailing traffic increased on the lake after the war; and by the early 1780s, the British had placed a beacon on top of the fort.

The purpose of the light was to prevent vessels sailing at night from running too far westward of Fort Niagara. A light is believed to have been kept in the tower only when a vessel was expected. Within a few years after the newly independent United States of America occupied Fort Niagara, in 1796, the fortress lighthouse was discontinued. The tower atop the fort is shown in drawings of the structure as late as 1803, but by 1806 it was gone.

Not until 1823 did another beacon, with a wooden tower, go into service atop the old French Castle. But two years later the Erie Canal was opened, and most of the river's east–west traffic was diverted away from the old Niagara Portage. The final blow to the commercial importance of the Niagara Portage came in 1829, when Canada opened its Welland Canal and commerce westward to the fast-growing city of Buffalo, on Lake Erie. Still, there was enough ship traffic on the Lake Ontario side of the Niagara River to warrant a light.

By the 1870s the Army began to find the light's location an inconvenience to daily life at the fort. It was abandoned in 1872, when a fifty-foot, octagonal stone tower was completed on the shore of Lake Ontario just south of the fort. In 1900 a lamp-oil shed was built and the tower was raised eleven feet to make the light visible twenty-five miles out onto Lake Ontario. The additional tower space was used to house a watch room, which included a built-in desk for the keeper.

Edward Giddings, keeper of the light during the 1820s, figured in the William Morgan Affair, a major political incident. Giddings and others were suspected of having murdered Morgan, a disgruntled Freemason who had threatened to reveal Masonic secret rites to the public. Shortly before he disappeared in 1826, Morgan was held by the Army at Fort Niagara, perhaps with the connivance of Giddings. News of this leaked to the press, precipitating a national scandal. Rumors of dark Masonic conspiracies could be heard on any street corner. Taking advantage of the furor, a small group of enterprising politicians founded the Anti-Masonic Party, an ephemeral player in the grand game of American national politics. As it turned out, the party was not so much anti-Masonic as it was anti-Andrew Jackson, who was then president of the United States as well as a Freemason. Ironically, William Wirt, the Anti-Masonic Party's presidential candidate in 1832, was himself a Freemason. He was soundly defeated by his fellow Freemason Jackson.

HOW TO GET THERE:

The attractions of Niagara Falls are ample and legendary, but visitors interested in human as well as natural history should set aside time for a trip to nearby Old Fort Niagara State Park.

The fort has served three nations and stands as a memorial to the grit and persistence of those who explored, fought for, and settled the new world. There are living-history exhibits and numerous military reenactments during the summer.

The fort is open from mid-April through Labor Day, while the lighthouse is open weekends in June and then daily through Labor Day. Admission to the park and lighthouse exhibit is free. From Niagara, New York, follow the Robert Moses Parkway to the park entrance. Once inside the park, follow the signs to the lighthouse (recently deactivated by the Coast Guard). For more information call (716) 745–7611.

B uilt in 1877, the Vermilion Lighthouse served until 1929, the year of the great stock-market crash on Wall Street. Half a century of Lake Erie storms had left the tower and its foundation in such a sad state of repair that the Lighthouse Service demolished the structure rather than allow it to collapse. More than sixty years passed before a local fund-raising effort made possible construction of the tower shown here, a replica of the original. The lighthouse was completed in 1991. Today it is a key attraction of the adjacent Inland Seas Maritime Museum. The lighthouse and museum are located at the end Main Street, about 3 blocks north of U.S. 6 in Vermilion, Ohio. For more information call the Vermilion Historical Society at (216) 967–3467.

CHAPTER TWO

Lights of
THE WARRIOR LAKE
ERIE

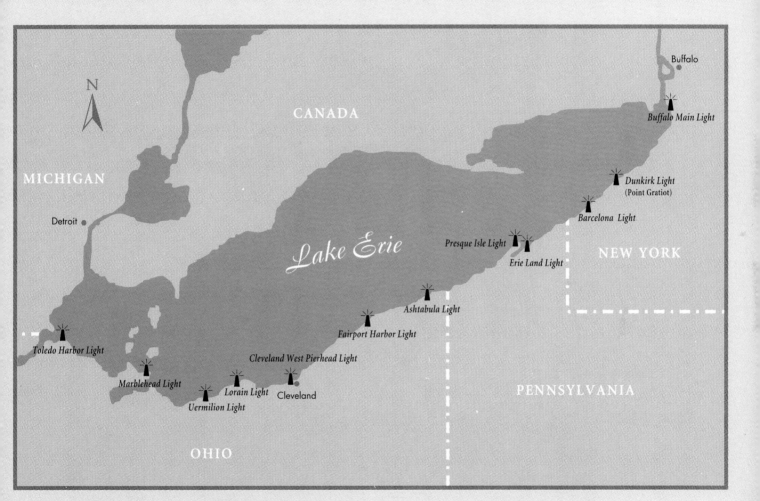

Buffalo

Buffalo Main Light

CANADA

Dunkirk Light
(Point Gratiot)

MICHIGAN

Barcelona Light

Detroit

Presque Isle Light

NEW YORK

Lake Erie

Erie Land Light

Ashtabula Light

Fairport Harbor Light

Toledo Harbor Light

Cleveland West Pierhead Light

Marblehead Light

PENNSYLVANIA

Lorain Light

Cleveland

Uermilion Light

OHIO

This harbor light station in Buffalo, pictured here as it appeared in 1914, is no longer standing. (Courtesy National Archives)

Generally speaking, lighthouses serve the mariners of all nations. But because they are built and maintained by governments, lighthouses are closely linked to political history. They have played important roles in the prosecution of war and in the making of nations.

As a builder of lighthouses, the United States is a world leader. We have more lighthouses along our inland shores (the shores of the Great Lakes) than most nations have on their entire ocean coastlines. This might not have been true, though, except for a rare freshwater naval battle fought more than 180 years ago.

BUCKSKINS *and* TOMAHAWKS

On a September afternoon in 1813, backwoodsmen and farmers living in the remote northwestern corner of Ohio might have thought a storm had broken far out over the waters of Lake Erie. So it had, but the booming that they heard in the distance was no natural thunder. Rather, it was the roar of cannon, and the "storm" was a mighty sea battle being fought nearly 500 miles from the nearest salt water. Somewhere out there on the lake, a flotilla of heavily armed American warships and an equally powerful British fleet were slugging it out with steel and lead for control of Lake Erie and of the entire Great Lakes region.

One of only a very few naval engagements ever fought in freshwater, this extraordinary confrontation also proved to have been one of history's most decisive battles. The chain of events leading up to the Battle of Lake Erie began in a most unlikely way: with a bloody musket-and-tomahawk clash between buckskinned frontiersmen and Indians in war paint. In 1811 an army of pioneers, commanded by a flamboyant general named William Henry Harrison, ran head-on into a large Indian war party led by the legendary Tecumseh and his brother, "The Prophet." The battle erupted along an otherwise placid Indiana creek known to the Indians as Tippecanoe. When it was over, Tecumseh and his braves had been driven off, leaving behind many dead and a considerable number of British muskets.

Harrison's victory left an indelible mark on history. It opened up the midwestern states of Ohio, Indiana, and Illinois to a flood of white settlers, who now felt relatively safe from the Indians. It launched Harrison on a successful military and political career, which thirty years afterward would land him in the White House as the ninth president of the United States. In fact, Harrison campaigned for the presidency on the slogan "Tippecanoe and Tyler Too," a phrase that, to this day, still twists the tongues of grammar-school history students. But the battle's most immediate effect was to inflame American public opinion against the British, who were accused of supplying weapons to hostile western tribes. The anti-British sentiment grew to such a fever pitch that war was declared the following summer.

The decision to make war on the world's dominant naval power would quickly prove a disastrous one. The British swept American shipping from the seas, sealed off eastern ports, and even burned the White House and the Capitol in Washington, D.C. Except for a brash twenty-eight-year-old naval lieutenant and his ragtag fleet on Lake Erie, the British might also have snatched away the vast lands to the south and west of the Great Lakes and given them to Canada.

When Lieutenant Oliver Hazard Perry arrived in Ohio during the autumn of 1812, he had no ships to command. His assignment of driving an already established British fleet from Lake Erie

An unexpected shift in the weather? Killer storms can strike suddenly on the Great Lakes, throwing up towering waves as dangerous as any on the open ocean.

seemed hopeless. Perry's warships had to be built from scratch, using raw timber felled right on the shores of the lake.

As his small party of shipwrights and seamen labored around the clock, Perry kept a wary eye on the lakeward horizon. He was watching for sails signaling the British attack that he was sure was coming to burn his unfinished ships, destroy his makeshift shipyard, and scatter his tiny force into the wilderness. But as construction of the American fleet continued, month after weary month, the British held back.

Commanding the British naval forces on the lake was Captain Robert Barclay, a veteran of the famed Battle of Trafalgar. Barclay felt secure at his base in Detroit, Michigan, and perhaps he took his young opponent too lightly. For whatever reason Barclay never attacked; and by the summer of 1813, Perry was able to complete and launch eight ships.

Early in September the American commander made his move. Having sailed his small fleet to the west end of Lake Erie, Perry blockaded the mouth of the Detroit River and cut off British supplies. Soon Barclay was forced to sail out and meet Perry on the open waters of the lake.

WE HAVE MET *the* ENEMY

The battle, fought just to the west of Put-in-Bay and north of what is today the city of Sandusky, Ohio, commenced shortly before noon on September 10. The British cannon had longer range and began to blast away before the American ships could reply. But a favorable shift in the wind brought the two lines of embattled ships close together and allowed Perry's heavier short-range cannon to pound the enemy. Perry had filled the rigging of his largest vessels, the *Lawrence* and *Niagara,* with Kentucky long-riflemen, and their hawk-eyed sharpshooting picked off key British officers one by one. Although he would survive the battle, even Barclay fell, seriously wounded, on the deck of his flagship, the *Detroit.* By mid-afternoon the British were forced to strike their colors, and Perry, who would forever after be known as "Commodore Perry," was able to send his famous message back to the American shores: "We have met the enemy and they are ours; two ships, two brigs, one schooner, and one sloop."

Destruction of Barclay's fleet made it possible for General Harrison to march on Detroit and clear American territory of British outposts. In October he defeated the retreating British and their Indian allies, in a bitterly contested battle on Canadian soil. The entire British force was either killed or captured, and the charismatic Tecumseh was cut down while making a stubborn last stand with his braves.

Harrison's success on land, combined with Perry's victory out on Lake Erie, likely saved the Great Lakes states for the Americans. Without those states and the access to vital inland waterways that they provided, the United States certainly would have been a much different, and poorer, country. By 1841, when Harrison became president, commerce generated by the Great Lakes region was already producing an economic boom. The Erie Canal linked the lakes to the Hudson and the Atlantic Seaboard while a growing string of lighthouses led freighters and passenger steamers from Buffalo to Detroit and beyond.

As president, Harrison might have pushed for even more economic growth in the lakes region—perhaps ordering the construction of additional lighthouses—but he never got the chance. It rained on the day he took the oath of office. Sixty-seven and in fragile health, Harrison was no longer the robust frontier soldier that he had been during the War of 1812. While making what turned out to be the longest inauguration speech in history, he caught a severe cold. Ironically, little more than a month after taking office, the hero of Tippecanoe died from a fatal case of the sniffles.

Beauty, history, and function combine in this fine old ship's wheel gracing the maritime museum of Fairport Lighthouse in Ohio. Such treats await visitors to lighthouse museums throughout the Great Lakes region.

BUFFALO MAIN LIGHT

Buffalo, New York – 1818 and 1833

With the opening of the Erie Canal in 1825, Buffalo began a hurly-burly boom that lasted well into the twentieth century and made this city near the eastern end of Lake Erie one of the busiest ports in the world. Political leaders had long recognized the commercial and strategic importance of the place. A light was planned for Buffalo's harbor as early as 1805, when Congress designated the village a port of entry. But action was delayed by tight-fisted New York legislators, who refused to share the cost of construction; and then by the British, who burned Buffalo during the War of 1812.

The Buffalo Main Lighthouse was finally completed and placed in operation in 1818, in tandem with the light at Erie, Pennsylvania, known then as Presque Isle. These were the first two U.S. government lights on Lake Erie. A new, more powerful lighthouse was completed in 1833. Built at the end of a 1,400-foot-long pier, the buff-colored, octagonal limestone tower rose sixty-eight feet above the lake. By 1872 a major breakwater light station was in operation at the end of a recently completed 4,000-foot-long breakwater. The breakwater light was fitted with a fourth-order fixed red light; and the fog bell (later to be replaced by a steam whistle) was moved from the main light to the new breakwater station.

A successful fund drive to restore the 1833 tower was begun in the early 1960s, and in 1985 the newly formed Buffalo Lighthouse Association began the project. In 1987 a replacement lens was lit in the restored tower for the city's first International Friendship Festival.

HOW TO GET THERE:

Overlooking the terminus of the Erie Canal, the Buffalo Lighthouse is located on the grounds of a Coast Guard station and is probably best viewed from the Naval and Serviceman's Park, just across the river in downtown Buffalo. To reach the lighthouse, take I–190 to the Church Street exit, then turn right at the first stoplight onto Lower Terrace. Follow the signs to the Erie Basin Marina and Buffalo Main Lighthouse. For additional information call (716) 947–9126.

The Buffalo Main Lighthouse, bearing its date of construction, still stands. Notice the bottle light in the background.

DUNKIRK (POINT GRATIOT) LIGHT

Point Gratiot, New York – 1829 and 1875

Dunkirk Lighthouse rises from a twenty-foot-high bluff at Point Gratiot, southwest of the Erie Canal terminus in Buffalo. Today it still throws its guiding beam across Lake Erie, just as it once did for nineteenth-century immigrant ships bound for the upper Great Lakes. Although its light helped keep vessels on course, it could not always prevent tragedy.

The first light at Dunkirk Harbor was commissioned in 1826, only a few years after one of the earliest recorded disasters on eastern Lake Erie. Launched in 1818 at Black Rock, New York, the paddlewheeler *Walk-In-The-Water* was the lake's first steamboat. But the power of steam could not altogether overcome the forces of nature, and in October 1818 this famous steamboat foundered on a sandbar in heavy weather.

The 132-foot-long, thirty-two-foot-beam *Walk-In-The-Water* was en route from Buffalo and Detroit with a load of passengers and freight. Passage on the one-and-a-half-day cruise was eighteen dollars for a cabin and seven dollars for steerage. This particular trip turned out not to be such a bargain; but, luckily, all the passengers were saved. Even the ship's huge steam engine was salvaged.

In 1841 the *Erie*, bound from Buffalo to Chicago, burned, with the loss of 141 lives, three miles east of Dunkirk. The tragedy was blamed on painters who had

A glowing Fresnel lens at Dunkirk Lighthouse on Point Gratiot competes with the setting sun.

placed demijohns of turpentine and varnish on the deck immediately above the *Erie's* boilers. The painters were riding the vessel as far as Erie, Pennsylvania, where they had a contract to paint the vessel SS *Madison*. In addition to her crew of thirty, the *Erie* carried 140 German and Swiss immigrants. The steamboat *De Witt Clinton*, which had just left Dunkirk, rescued twenty-seven survivors.

On October 14, 1893, the wooden steamboat *Dean Richmond*, named for a railway builder, foundered in heavy weather near Dunkirk. Built in Cleveland in 1864, the *Dean Richmond* made regular runs between Buffalo and Chicago. She left her last port of call— Toledo, Ohio—on October 13, 1893, with a cargo of bagged meal and flour, copper sheets, $50,000 worth of pig zinc, and $141,000 in gold and silver bullion. Gale-force winds battered her as she steamed eastward, and the unsecured copper sheets stowed on deck began to shift. The *Richmond* is believed to have tried to run in to Dunkirk just before she sank. Area residents, including the keeper of the Dunkirk Lighthouse and his family, managed to salvage hundreds of bags of damp flour following the wreck. It is said that, when the flour dried out, it made perfectly good bread.

The loss of the freighter *Idaho* off Dunkirk, during the late fall of 1897, brought a different sort of bounty to the area. The ship was carrying a large load of merchandise intended to be sold as Christmas presents, including a hefty store of chocolate, which washed ashore in large slabs. (No doubt children hereabouts had a very sweet Christmas that year.)

The first lighthouse at Gratiot Point, which became popularly known as Lighthouse Point, was completed in 1826 by Buffalo contractor Jesse Peck. It stood a short distance from the current sixty-one-foot-high tower, which replaced it in 1875.

Early attempts were made here to substitute natural gas for the whale oil typically used to fuel lighthouse lamps. These experiments were not successful, however. In 1857 the lantern was fitted with a third-order Fresnel lens, which produced a 15,000-candlepower flash every ninety seconds. The light could be seen from seventeen miles offshore.

Today the light station at Point Gratiot serves as a military memorial as well as a lighthouse museum. Point Gratiot is believed to be named for Charles Gratiot, the same U.S. Army engineer for whom Fort Gratiot, on Michigan's St. Clair River, is named.

HOW TO GET THERE:

The lighthouse complex, which included one of the famous bottle lights from Buffalo, is open daily from April through November and at other times upon request. The seven-room keeper's house now serves as one of the best lighthouse museums on the Great Lakes. Special events include War of 1812 reenactments, craft shows, and even lighthouse moonlight cruises. For details call (716) 366–5050. The lighthouse is located in Dunkirk just off Route 5, which parallels the lakeshore just northwest of the New York State Thruway (I–90).

BARCELONA LIGHT

Barcelona, New York – 1829

Built in 1829 near a natural-gas–emitting spring, Barcelona Lighthouse became the first public building in the United States to be illuminated by gas. It is believed to have been the only lighthouse in the world ever to have been lighted with natural gas. Otherwise, the station had a short-lived and not overly distinctive career.

In 1828 Congress appropriated $5,000 to build a lighthouse on a bluff at what was then known as Portland Harbor, a community about twenty miles west of Dunkirk, New York. Completed the following year, it was fitted with oil lamps and a fourteen-inch reflector.

Three years later settlers in the area made an astonishing discovery: a pool of water that would, on occasion, catch fire. This "burning spring" produced natural gas, and inventive local folk soon found a way to put it to work. Placing a masonry cap over the gas well, they used wooden pipes to move the gas to the new Barcelona lighthouse. At the top of the tower, the gas was burned in specially designed lamps. The flame was so intense that it seemed to some sailors out on Lake Erie that the whole lighthouse was aflame. This rustic technology worked well enough for several years, but then the flow from the gas well began to falter. After 1838 the well produced gas only sporadi-

cally, and the keeper was forced to use oil lamps instead.

The lighthouse was discontinued in 1859, when the government discovered a rather embarrassing error. The light had been intended to guide vessels into Barcelona's harbor. It was a good plan, but the fact was, Barcelona had no harbor. In time the Lighthouse Board sold the lighthouse for use as a private home.

Made of split native fieldstone, the forty-foot-high conical tower still stands. The tower and keeper's cottage are so attractive that they are often depicted on postcards. That they have survived the years speaks well for their Early American workmanship. The cottage has stone walls twenty inches thick. According to the original specifications, the inside woodwork was "to be finished in a plain, decent style with good seasoned stuff."

Its light extinguished before the Civil War, the stone tower of Barcelona Lighthouse still stands. The lantern was removed long ago, but the owners added a wooden framework at the top to suggest the tower's original function.

HOW TO GET THERE:

Located just off I–90 on East Lake Road (Route 5) in Bar-celona, the lighthouse is a private residence and not open to the public. Visitors are reminded not to trespass but to enjoy the lighthouse from the public right-of-way. Although the lantern was removed more than a century ago, a wooden-frame structure now simulates the lantern.

PRESQUE ISLE LIGHT

Erie, Pennsylvania – 1819, 1867, and 1873

Originally, Pennsylvania had no shore frontage on Lake Erie, but the farsighted people of that friendly state recognized the importance of access to America's strategic inland seas. So, immediately after the Revolutionary War, they bought a forty-five-mile stretch of beaches and inlets, including what turned out to be a very attractive and historic harbor. It was at Erie, Pennsylvania, that Perry and his shipwrights built the modest flotilla of warships that defeated the powerful Great Lakes fleet of the British during the War of 1812.

Perhaps it was partly in memory of that victory, as well as in recognition of the growing importance of Erie as a port, that the government built the nation's second Great Lakes lighthouse in Pennsylvania. The light was placed on the Presque Isle Peninsula in 1819, to mark the entrance to Erie Bay. In French, the term *presque isle* means "not an island," and in this case it apparently refers to the long, narrow peninsula. Shortly after the Civil War, this early lighthouse was replaced by a stately sandstone tower, which served lake sailors from 1867 until it was permanently discontinued in 1897. The old tower can still be seen in Erie's Dunn Park. Unfortunately, its original lantern room and dwelling were removed long ago.

The structure, known today as Presque Isle Light Station, was completed during the summer of 1873. It was fitted with a fourth-order Fresnel lens displaying a fixed white light. The sixty-eight-foot square tower placed the focal plane of the light seventy-three feet above the lake surface. The Fresnel lens has been replaced by an automated, airport–style beacon.

HOW TO GET THERE:

The active Presque Isle Lighthouse stands in Presque Isle State Park, at the end of a 7-mile-long finger of sand stretching into Lake Erie. From I–79, take Pennsylvania Alternate Route 5 west. At the fourth street light, turn right onto Route 832 (Peninsula Drive) and continue north 1½ miles to the park entrance. The lighthouse is located about 3 miles from the entrance. The restored Erie Land Lighthouse is located in Dunn Park. To reach the park, follow Lake Road East about ½ mile beyond East Avenue, and then turn toward Lake Erie onto Lighthouse Street.

The Erie Land Lighthouse, erected in 1818 during the presidency of James Monroe, was among the first light towers on the Great Lakes. Unfortunately, construction crews failed to heed the biblical warning not to "build on sinking sand," and the tower leaned queasily out of plumb. Eventually, it was torn down and, in 1867, replaced by the sandstone tower seen today. Abandoned in 1899, its lantern room was lopped off, making it a headless giant. Thanks to the efforts of local citizens and government financing, the venerable structure was recently restored to its original appearance. (Courtesy Bob and Sandra Shanklin)

Positioned at the tip of a long breakwater, Ashtabula Lighthouse has marked the entrance to the harbor at Ashtabula, Ohio, since 1916. Earlier lighthouses guided ships here as far back as 1835. A good view of the lighthouse can be had from Point Park, near the intersection of Walnut and Hulbert streets, in the Ashtabula waterfront district. Across from the park is the Great Lakes Marine and U.S. Coast Guard Memorial Museum, a must for anyone interested in the history of commerce, lifesaving, and lighthouses on the lakes. The museum is open on weekend and holiday afternoons from June through October. For more information call (216) 964–6847. (Courtesy Gordon D. Amsbary)

FAIRPORT HARBOR LIGHT

Fairport, Ohio – 1825

Fairport Harbor, located midway between Cleveland and Ashtabula, was once the gateway to the old Western Reserve, owned by the state of Connecticut. Fairport's importance to Great Lakes shipping increased after 1803, when the new state of Ohio was formed from land relinquished by Connecticut and Virginia.

For countless immigrants bound for Michigan, Wisconsin, and Minnesota, the Fairport Harbor Light provided the first welcome glimpse of the American Midwest. Fairport long served as a refueling and supply port for passenger vessels and freighters bound westward from Buffalo, New York. The harbor's peak year before the Civil War was 1847, when 2,987 vessels transited the port, carrying $991,000 in cargo and an unknown number of passengers. The principal imports were farm wagons, furniture, cheese, flour, oil of peppermint, and, of course, people.

The light station at Fairport was completed in the fall of 1825, the same year that the Erie Canal opened, connecting the Great Lakes with the Hudson River and the port of New York. Fairport's first lighthouse was built on the east side of the Grand River by Jonathan Goldsmith, a Connecticut native who had moved to Ohio in 1811. Goldsmith was awarded the contract for the lighthouse by A. W. Walworth, collector of customs for the district of Cuyahoga at Cleveland. A resident of Fairport, Walworth's father had been one of the earliest settlers of the Western Reserve. The senior Walworth had swapped houses with a Cleveland resident who believed that Fairport, not Cleveland, would be the area's major city.

The original brick tower was thirty feet high, with supporting walls three feet thick at the ground and twenty inches thick at the top. The tower was given an eleven-foot-diameter soapstone deck and capped with an octagonal-shaped iron lantern. The two-story keeper's house had spacious rooms, each with plastered walls, three windows, and a fireplace. There were also a sizable kitchen and cellar. The first keeper to live and work here was Samuel Butler.

By mid-century both the tower and keeper's cottage had badly deteriorated, and in 1869 Congress appropriated $30,000 to replace them. By August 1871 the station's third-order Fresnel lens had been installed in a new sandstone tower, where it shined for more than half a century.

On June 9, 1925, a new combination light and foghorn station was put in operation, and the federal government announced that it would raze the old lighthouse. Local appeals to save the historic structure succeeded, and in 1941 the village of Fairport leased the lighthouse from the Coast Guard. Today the Fairport Harbor Historical Society maintains the lighthouse as a marine museum.

HOW TO GET THERE:

The museum in the old keeper's dwelling includes a wonderful collection of artifacts from the early days of the Lighthouse Service and a variety of other maritime exhibits. The museum is open from 1:00 to 6:00 P.M. on Wednesday, Saturday, Sunday, and legal holidays from Memorial Day through Labor Day. For more information call (216) 354–4825. The museum is located at the northwest corner of Second and High streets in the village of Fairport Harbor. From U.S. 20 at Painesville, follow either Route 283 or Route 535 to the village.

WEST PIERHEAD LIGHT

Cleveland, Ohio – ca. 1910

Cleveland, Ohio's, West Pierhead Lighthouse marks the entrance to the navigable Cuyahoga River and to the city's bustling inner harbor. As well known to freighter captains as any lighthouse on the Great Lakes, it is also a familiar and well-loved feature of the Cleveland waterfront.

Standing on a thick concrete-and-stone foundation, which lifts it well above lake level, the station consists of a thirty-foot brick tower with a connected steel foghorn building. Both structures are painted white and trimmed in green. Two rings of portholes give the tower a distinctly nautical appearance. Floodlights illuminate the lighthouse at night, making it a bright centerpiece of the evening harborscape.

A one-story minitower and lantern room sit atop the main tower. The light, visible for ten miles, is provided by a fourth-order Fresnel lens and reaches onto the lake from a point sixty-three feet above the water.

The foghorn building once contained a steam-powered signaling device, which made a deep-throated sound something like the lowing of a cow. Consequently, the horn was known to mariners and Cleveland residents alike as "the cow." Lake sailors may have laughed at the sound it made, but no few of them owed their lives to its guidance. It could be heard from up to twelve miles away in a dense fog.

About half a mile across the harbor entrance, the thirty-foot tower of the Cleveland East Pierhead Lighthouse stands on a circular platform protected by a low wall of steel and stone. This small tower guards the tip of an extensive breakwater that forms the Cleveland inner harbor and helps protect the shoreline from storm-driven waves. Both the East and West Pierhead Lighthouses date to about 1910.

(Courtesy U.S. Coast Guard / W. C. Helbig)

HOW TO GET THERE:

From I–90 in downtown Cleveland, take the Ohio Highway 2 exit and drive west about 1 mile to the Ninth Street exit. Turn right, follow Ninth Street for about 2 blocks, and park in the lot beside the harbor. The lighthouses can be seen from many points along the waterfront, but harbor cruises offer the best views. Several cruises are available daily aboard the Goodtime III, berthed near the harbor parking area. For information on cruises call (216) 861–5110. Also near the parking area is a pair of museum ships, the steam freighter William G. Mather and the USS Cod, a World War II submarine. The Cod survived seven combat missions in the Pacific and sank forty Japanese ships.

LORAIN LIGHT

Lorain, Ohio – 1917

Seldom is a town so closely identified with its lighthouse as Lorain, Ohio. "It's our symbol," said one longtime resident. "New York City has the Statue of Liberty, and we have our lighthouse."

Indeed, the lighthouse is celebrated all over Lorain. Its likeness emblazons napkins and placemats in restaurants. It shows up in murals on the walls of public buildings, on the covers of community telephone books, and on calendars handed out by banks. It can even be seen on the membership pins of Lorain Lions Club members. Luckily for those of us who love lighthouses, the real thing can also still be seen, standing on its massive, square concrete foundation at the end of a long harbor breakwater. Except for a series of October storms

The citizens of Lorain, Ohio, are so fond of their lighthouse that they fought a five-year battle with government officials to save it. The Coast Guard had planned to demolish the structure after an automated breakwater light went into service in 1965. Together with a series of well-timed Lake Erie storms that delayed the wrecking operation, a wave of community support for the old lighthouse saved it from destruction. With its shutters and pitched roof, the building looks like an old-fashioned town home. Instead, it is a fortresslike shell of concrete and steel, capable of withstanding the worst weather the lake can throw at it.
(Courtesy David Kramer)

on Lake Erie—and for some fast work on the part of local preservationists—the grand old lighthouse would have disappeared more than thirty years ago.

For at least 150 years, lights have guided vessels to Lorain. During the early 1800s this purpose was served in a modest, makeshift manner, by a lantern hung from a pole. But by 1837 the town had its own official lighthouse: a wooden tower rising from the end of a harbor pier. The lamps at the top of the tower burned lard oil and must have been darkened frequently by soot.

In 1917 the Army Corps of Engineers built the lighthouse seen at Lorain today. Like so many other things made by the Corps, famous for building dams and bridges, this lighthouse was meant to last. The engineers poured hundreds of tons of concrete and fill into the foundation so that it could resist the huge waves thrown at it by Lake Erie storms. They gave it concrete-and-steel walls ten inches thick. In short, they built a structure more like a fortress than a lighthouse.

Even so, shuttered windows and a pitched roof lent the building a homey appearance, not unlike that of residences in the town. Into one corner, a square tower extended only a few feet above the red-tiled roof. Perched atop the tower, a small, cast-iron lantern room with diamond-shaped windows housed a rotating fourth-order Fresnel lens. Recurring every ten seconds, flashes from the lens could be seen from fifteen miles out on the lake.

The Lorain Lighthouse performed its nightly task without interruption for almost half a century. Then, in 1965, a small, fully automated light tower was established at the tip of a recently constructed breakwater. The U.S. Coast Guard decommissioned the old lighthouse and approved a contract to have it demolished.

As it turned out, the people of Lorain had great affection for their lighthouse. A committee of concerned citizens formed to save the structure, but their efforts would have come too late except for a series of prodigious October storms, which held the wrecking crews at bay. By the time the angry lake calmed down, winter had set in, giving the committee a chance to raise funds and lobby Congress. Eventually, this hard work paid off, and the lighthouse was saved.

The Lorain Lighthouse recently survived another threat—this time from the lake itself. Decades of storms such as the ones that helped save the structure in 1965 had seriously weakened the foundation. In 1994 the Army Corps of Engineers, which had built the lighthouse in first place, now stepped in to save it. To stabilize the foundation. the Corps pumped in nearly 500 cubic yards of grout. This work was accompanied by a general facelift of the building, at a total cost of $850,000—more than twenty-four times the $35,000 that it took to build the lighthouse in 1917. The twentieth century has been hard on the value of the dollar and on lighthouses, but here is a lighthouse story with a happy ending. Although nowadays the Lorain Lighthouse primarily serves mariners as a daymark, it continues to shine as an inspiration to the people of the town.

HOW TO GET THERE:

From U.S. 6, turn north onto Oberlin Avenue and drive approximately 3 blocks to the parking area at the municipal pier. A good view of the lighthouse can be had from the north end of the parking area and from several other points along the Lake Erie shore.

MARBLEHEAD LIGHT

Bay Point, Ohio – 1821

uilt in 1821, Marblehead Lighthouse can boast the oldest active light tower on the Great Lakes. The Marblehead beacon has flashed out over a lot of history since it was placed in service, only a few years after Perry won his decisive victory over the British at the Battle of Lake Erie. This key naval battle was fought only a few miles to the north of Marblehead in September 1813, but that was not the last time that war would touch the area.

During the Civil War more than 10,000 Confederate soldiers languished in a 300-acre prison on Johnson's Island, within sight of the Marblehead Light. Most of the prisoners were officers captured in battles far to the south. No doubt these men frequently

The solid stone beach at the foot of Marblehead Lighthouse makes it easy to understand how this place got its name. Homesick Confederates in a nearby Civil War prison camp could see the light shining in this tower.

dreamed of their homes and farms in far-off Dixie; but few, if any, ever escaped. At least one daring attempt, however, was made to free them.

On September 18, 1864, a small band of Confederate partisans commandeered the passenger steamer *Parsons* and headed for Johnson's Island. Apparently, they hoped to free some or all of the thousands of Confederate prisoners held there. Along the way the pirates encountered a second steamer, the *Island Queen,* and, after a blazing gun battle, overwhelmed its crew. The *Island Queen* was set adrift, and the passengers and crew from both vessels were put ashore on remote Middle Bass Island. Now the *Parsons* became what might be described as the only Confederate warship ever to serve on the Great Lakes. Unfortunately for the Southerners, the *Parsons* came up against the powerful Union gunboat *Michigan,* guarding the approach to Johnson's Island. Unable to challenge the *Michigan*'s heavy cannon, the Confederates scuttled the steamer and escaped into Canada.

The Confederate prisoners on Johnson's Island may never have learned of the effort to free them. One thing they did learn, though, was the new sport of baseball. Residents of nearby Ohio communities taught them the rules. The Southerners proved very good at the game, regularly defeating Yankee teams who visited the island to play them. When they returned to the South following the war, the former prisoners took the sport with them. No doubt they also carried memories of their long imprisonment and of a light flashing every night on the shore as if to call them home.

The light they saw was, of course, the beacon of Marblehead Lighthouse, which over one and three-quarters centuries has called countless thousands of sailors home from the lake. During all that time the old stone tower has changed very little. Late in the nineteenth century, its height was raised from fifty-five to sixty-five feet, but otherwise it looks much as it has since 1821. Fitted with a fourth-order Fresnel lens, it displays a flashing green light.

HOW TO GET THERE:

From Highway 2 at Port Clinton, take Route 163 to Marblehead. The light can be seen from a convenient parking area. The keeper's dwelling is used as a museum by the Ottawa County Historical Society. The grounds overlook the entrance to historic Sandusky Bay. For hours and other information, call the Ottawa County Visitors Bureau at (419) 734–4386.

TOLEDO HARBOR LIGHT

Toledo, Ohio – 1904

Mariners seeing the Toledo Harbor Lighthouse for the first time or watching as it emerges mysteriously from one of Lake Erie's thick fog banks must rub their eyes and look again. Chocolate-colored brick walls, Romanesque arches, and a bulging round-edge roof make this lighthouse an architectural wonder. It is hard to say exactly what storybook fantasy the structure was intended to suggest—perhaps part-Victorian-palace and part-Russian-Orthodox-church. But for all its fancifulness, the old lighthouse is a hard-working lake veteran: It has served faithfully since 1904.

Shortly before the turn of the century, the Army Corps of Engineers dredged a channel from Lake Erie into the Maumee River. This opened Toledo to an influx of deepwater freighter traffic. To mark the channel and point the way to the city's busy harbor, the Corps built a lighthouse about eight miles out in the lake from Toledo. The design was, no doubt, some military engineer's concept of a stylish building.

With their usual zeal for solid construction, the corpsmen established the structure on a massive concrete-and-stone crib rising almost twenty feet above the water. They gave it stout brick walls three stories high and pushed the light tower up through the center of the roof. They fitted the lantern room atop the tower with a state-of-the-art, rotating Fresnel lens. With a focal plane more than seventy feet above the lake, the Fresnel's alternating red-and-white flashes could be seen from sixteen miles away. Although automated since 1965, the station remains active.

Like many other old lighthouses around the country, this one is said to be haunted. Considering the look of the place, it would be surprising if the building were *not* haunted. Some say, however, that the stories of a phantom can be traced to U.S. Coast Guard efforts to discourage vandalism at the station. Following removal of the last keeper in 1965, the Coast Guard placed a fully uniformed mannequin in one of the lower windows to serve as a scarecrow.

HOW TO GET THERE:

The only satisfactory way to see the lighthouse is from a boat, as the station is off-limits to visitors. The light's distinctive red-and-white flash, however, can be seen from many points along the Toledo shoreline.

(Courtesy U.S. Coast Guard)

The Cheboygan Crib Lighthouse (at right) stands at the end of a short pier. It was once located off-shore nearby, but the concrete-and-stone crib on which it stood settled into the lake, rendering it useless. The town of Cheboygan salvaged the old light and placed it on display in an attractive park at the end of Huron Street, east from U.S. 23. From the pier, you can also see the Poe Reef Lighthouse. Round Island Light (above) once kept its lonely vigil at the end of a meandering sand spit. Other reef lighthouses are difficult to view from land, and none are open to the public.

CHAPTER THREE

Lights of
THE THUNDER LAKE
HURON

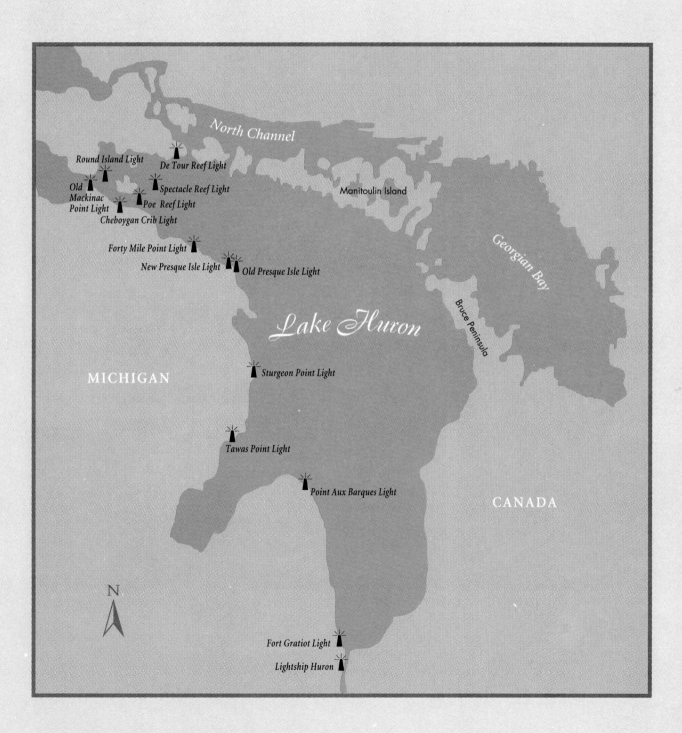

Round Island Light

De Tour Reef Light

North Channel

Manitoulin Island

Old Mackinac Point Light

Spectacle Reef Light

Poe Reef Light

Cheboygan Crib Light

Georgian Bay

Forty Mile Point Light

New Presque Isle Light

Old Presque Isle Light

Bruce Peninsula

Lake Huron

MICHIGAN

Sturgeon Point Light

Tawas Point Light

Point Aux Barques Light

CANADA

N

Fort Gratiot Light

Lightship Huron

DeTour Reef Lighthouse was built in 1931 over open water, as were all of Lake Huron's reef lighthouses. Cofferdams and mas-sive piers often had to be constructed first. (Courtesy National Archives)

*W*hy build lighthouses along the shores of the Great Lakes? For guidance. These lakes are no ordinary bodies of freshwater. They are enormous inland seas hundreds of miles in length. Sailors here need lighthouses to guide them, especially where low headlands offer few distinctive features. "It's like trying to navigate in a wheat field," said one frustrated sea captain after he brought his oceangoing freighter down the length of the St. Lawrence Seaway. But the Great Lakes lighthouses serve an even more important function: They save lives. On the wind-torn waters of these lakes, safety is a vitally important consideration, and sailors keep a close eye on the weather. In a storm, lighthouses provide mariners with a comforting visual anchor.

THE STORMS *of* NOVEMBER

November brings a marrow-deep chill to the bones of sailors on the Great Lakes. It's not just that the weather gets colder (it does, usually) but also that the lakes themselves take on a different character. They turn tempestuous and develop sharp, unpredictable tempers. Storms can blacken their faces in a matter of minutes and churn their waters into a confusion of towering waves capable of breaking a ship in half.

As the lakes change mood, so do the titanic commercial shipping enterprises they support. Captains and crews work overtime, hurrying to make one last trip; draw one last paycheck; or deliver one last cargo of iron, steel, oil, corn, or wheat before the witch of winter locks the lakes in a crush of unbreakable ice.

Tired sailors pushing themselves and their ships to the limit make a habit of looking back over their shoulders. They are watching for November—not the one on the calendar but the one that comes calling when you least expect it. Among Great Lakes sailors it is sometimes said that "Thanksgiving comes only if you survive November." They have endless tales of wreck and tragedy to prove the point: the November that took the *Fitzgerald* in 1975, the November that took the *Bradley* in 1958, and scores of other Novembers that sent stout ships and strong crews to the bottom. But when old lake sailors gather to tell stories of the calamities brought on by the year's eleventh month, there is one November they rarely leave out: November 1913.

Those who were superstitious about numbers said it would be an unlucky year; but up until the fall, 1913 had proved them wrong. The spring and summer had been kind to the Great Lakes, providing bathers, lovers, and sailors with a seemingly endless string of warm, clear days and calm, starry nights. Business was booming, and the large and growing fleet of freighters operating on the lakes set records for shipping.

Then came October and, with it, high winds howling out of the west. A record cold snap sent temperatures plunging below zero, and a series of early snowstorms dusted the lakes' shores with white. But for all its chill and bluster, October's unexpected outburst did little damage—a broken rudder here, a severed anchor chain there, and a couple of old wooden steamers run aground.

The year's fourth and final quarter had gotten off to an ominous start; but with lucrative contracts in their hands, captains were not willing to tie up their vessels for the season. They pushed themselves, their ships, and their crews harder than ever. They were determined to finish the work that they had begun in the spring and continued so successfully during the summer, attempting to make 1913 the best year ever for shipping on the Great Lakes. But it was not to be.

At first November seemed likely to reverse the unsettling trend of the previous month. For a week gentle breezes rippled the lakes, and the temperatures were downright balmy. But experienced sailors knew these pleasant conditions would not hold for long, not at this time of year; and how right they were. Even as they hung up their uniform jackets to enjoy the unseasonable temperatures in shirt-sleeves while their freighters cut through glass-smooth water, three deadly weather systems were headed their way. One rushed in with freezing winds from the Bering Sea; another poured over the Rockies, carrying an immense load of water from as far off as the South Pacific; and a third came spinning up, cyclone style, from the Caribbean. The three slammed into one another over the Great Lakes on or about November 7, 1913, creating what was in effect an inland hurricane.

This extraordinary storm struck with little or no warning. Dozens of freighters were caught in mid-lake, far from safe anchorage, or worse, near ship-killing rocks, shoals, and shallows. High waves battered hulls, and freezing spray caked decks and wheelhouses in a thick layer of ice. Swirling snow squalls blinded captains, pilots, and navigators, while high winds drove their vessels ever closer to disaster. The storm raged on without pause for five long days. By the time that the clouds broke and the winds died down, on November 12, more than forty ships had been wrecked, their hulls shattered by the waves or ripped open on shoals. Down with them went 235 sailors and passengers. Only a few of the bodies were ever recovered.

GOOD-BY NELLIE

On Lake Erie the 187-ton *Lightship No. 82* was blown off its mooring and bowled over by the waves. All six crewmen were lost. Before he drowned, Captain Hugh Williams apparently scratched a hurried farewell to his wife on a piece of wood and set it adrift. A waterlogged board later found washed up on a beach in New York held this message: "Good-by Nellie, ship breaking up fast. Williams."

Up on Lake Superior the tramp freighter *Leafield* was driven onto rocks and torn to pieces. All eighteen members of the crew were lost. Also lost on Superior was the 525-foot ore freighter *Henry B. Smith.* In a tragic lapse of judgment and prudent seamanship, Captain Jimmy Owen took the *Smith* out of the relative safety of Marquette Harbor and steamed directly into the teeth of the storm. Only a few scattered pieces of wreckage, and none of the ship's twenty-three crewmen, were ever found.

It was on Lake Huron, however, that the storm vented its full fury. When the storm first assaulted Huron on November 7, its shipping lanes were filled with vessels crossing northwestward toward Michigan and Superior or southeastward toward Erie. As darkness set in, lighthouse beacons called to these ships from many points along the Michigan shore. There were safe harbors in this storm, and the lights marked the way. But most ships could not reach them or make any headway at all against the fierce

westerly winds. Many captains pointed their bows toward the northeast and made a run for the Canadian side, where they hoped to find some protection. Many never made it.

Huron's mountainous waves chewed up dozens of ships, and the lake's deep waters swallowed them whole. At least eight large freighters—the *McGean, Carruthers, Hydrus, Wexford, Scott, Regina, Price,* and *Argus*—all disappeared from the lake without a trace. Vanishing with them were 178 passengers and crewmen.

Subzero winter temperatures can turn lake water as hard as concrete, which made it possible for this car to visit Poe Reef Lighthouse in 1937. (Courtesy U.S. Coast Guard)

LIGHTSHIP HURON

Port Huron, Michigan – 1921

Unlike the nearby Fort Gratiot Lighthouse, which has stood its ground for many years, the lightship *Huron* has had a highly mobile history. The keel for the *Huron* was laid by the Charles Seabury Company of Morris Heights, New York, in 1921, at the end of World War I. Commissioned as *Lightship No. 103* by the U.S. Lighthouse Service, it began its career as a relief lightship for Lake Michigan's Twelfth Lighthouse District. When other lightships had to be brought in for repairs, the *Huron* took over their station. After fourteen years of relief duty, *Lightship No. 103* was assigned first to Gray's Reef, Michigan, on Lake Michigan's east coast, and then to Manitou Shoals, on northern Lake Michigan. In 1935 the ninety-seven-foot vessel was placed on station at Corsica Shoals in Lake Huron, where it was a beacon for shipping bound to and from the St. Clair River.

At nights and in storms, the light from *Huron's* fifty-two-foot, six-inch-high lantern mast guided vessels into and out of the narrow, dredged channel, enabling large vessels to transit the river and lower Lake Huron. A 5,000-pound mushroom anchor kept the 310-ton, twenty-four-foot-beam lightship at her position, six miles north of the Blue Water Bridge over the St. Clair River in Port Huron and three miles east of the Michigan mainland.

In 1949 the lightship was refitted in Toledo, Ohio. The steam engine was replaced by diesels and radar, and a radio beacon and fog signal were added. Despite a 1945 Coast Guard directive that all lightship hulls be red, the *Huron* kept its black color. HURON was painted on its side in large block letters.

After being decommissioned in 1970, the *Huron* was acquired by the city of Port Huron. The lightship now serves as a museum, operated by the nearby Museum of Arts and History, with support from the Lake Huron Lore Marine Society. Nearby Fort Gratiot Light can be viewed from Lighthouse Park.

HOW TO GET THERE:

Enshrined since 1972 in Pine Grove Park in Port Huron, the lightship Huron *is open from 1:00 to 4:30 P.M. from Wednesday through Sunday in July and August and on weekends in May, June, and September. For information call (313) 982–0891. From I–94, drive south onto Pine Grove Street (M–25), turn left onto Prospect Street, and follow it 1 block to the lightship parking area. The* Huron *is located beside the water at the north end of Pine Grove Park.*

FORT GRATIOT LIGHT

Port Huron, Michigan – 1825 and 1829

Established in 1825, the Fort Gratiot Light Station is Michigan's oldest—older, in fact, than the state itself, which was admitted to the Union in 1837. Today, nearly one and three-quarters centuries after its light first guided sailors, the station still keeps watch over the Lake Huron entrance to the St. Clair River. Upstream is the lightship *Huron*, in Port Huron's Pine Grove Park. The last U.S. lightship to serve on the Great Lakes, it is a National Historic Landmark.

The first keeper of the Fort Gratiot Lighthouse was George McDougal, a Detroit lawyer who won his appointment through political influence. His was not a plum job, however, as McDougal depleted his personal savings keeping the station habitable. The tower was not built to government specifications, the materials used were shoddy, and McDougal considered it unsafe. He was correct. The tower fell down, and a more robust structure replaced it in 1829.

Today the tower stands eighty-two feet tall. Automated in 1933, its light has a focal plane eighty-six feet above lake level. The thick-walled, conical stone tower, overlaid with red brick, has been painted white. The keeper's cottage and fog-whistle house are red brick. Atop the tower a red dome covers the lantern room.

The Fort Gratiot Lighthouse is older than the state of Michigan itself. That's Canada in the background.

HOW TO GET THERE:

From I–94 take Pine Grove Street (M–25) north, then turn right onto Garfield Street and follow it to Gratiot Avenue. The lighthouse, open only a few times a year, is located on a Coast Guard facility. Parking is available in the area. For information on tours call (313) 982–0891 or ask at the nearby Huron Lightship Museum.

POINTE AUX BARQUES LIGHT

Port Austin, Michigan – 1848 and 1857

The French called the place *Pointe Aux Barques*, or "Point of Little Boats," perhaps because of the many canoes brought here by fur traders. This strategic headland marks a key turning point from Lake Huron into Saginaw Bay. Recognizing its importance to shipping, the federal government chose Pointe Aux Barques as the site for one of the tallest and most powerful lighthouses on the Great Lakes.

Completed in 1848 at a cost of $5,000, the original stone structure proved inadequate and had to be rebuilt less than ten years later. In 1857 it was replaced with an impressive eighty-nine-foot brick tower, fitted with a state-of-the-art, third-order Fresnel lens imported from France. Today this beautiful old lens can be seen at the Grice Museum in Port Austin. Its work is now being done by a 1 million-candle-power automated beacon. The flashing white light can be seen from about eighteen miles out on Lake Huron.

For many years Pointe Aux Barques also had an active lifesaving station. During the great November storm of 1913, the steamer *Howard M. Hanna* foundered near here. The station crew managed to save thirty-three of the *Hanna*'s passengers and crew. The station is now part of a very interesting museum complex in Huron City depicting life as it was lived here during the nineteenth century.

HOW TO GET THERE:

The Pointe Aux Barques Lighthouse is located in a county park off Lighthouse Road, about 10 miles east of Port Austin and 6 miles north of Port Hope. Take M–25 to Lighthouse Road. The keeper's dwelling houses a museum and gift shop, open on weekends from noon to 4:00 p.m. Memorial Day through Labor Day. The tower is not open to the public, but park visitors enjoy excellent views of the light. The park offers a campground and picnic area.

The Huron City Museum, with its many nineteenth-century displays and exhibits, is less than a mile to the northwest of the lighthouse and can be reached from M–25 via Huron City Road. Museum hours are 10:00 A.M. to 5:00 P.M. daily (except Tuesday) from July 1 through Labor Day. For information call (517) 428–4123.

As beautiful as it is useful, the Pointe Aux Barques Lighthouse still guides mariners. Its bright white tower makes an excellent daymark. As its French name suggests, this point has long been vital to shipping.

TAWAS POINT LIGHT

Tawas City, Michigan – 1853 and 1876

The thumb of Michigan's mitten is created by a long, southwestern extension of Lake Huron called Saginaw Bay. By the middle of the nineteenth century, the bay had become commercially strategic, and lighthouse officials saw the need to mark its entrance. In 1848 they placed a lighthouse at Pointe Aux Barques on the south side of the entrance, and five years later another was built at Ottawa Point (now known as Tawas Point) on the north side. The Tawas Point Lighthouse was completed and in operation by 1853, but its beacon served mariners for little more than twenty years.

Lake Huron constantly reshapes certain sections of its shoreline. By the 1870s sandy Tawas Point had grown so much that the lighthouse stood more than a mile from the waters of the lake. To correct this problem the Lighthouse Board asked Congress for a $30,000 appropriation to build a new lighthouse. The sixty-seven-foot tower was completed and in operation by 1876. The conical tower is painted white and is topped by a black-iron lantern room. The flashing white beacon is produced by a rotating fourth-order Fresnel lens.

To protect keepers from the weather, the brick dwelling was connected to the tower by a narrow brick passageway. Today the lighthouse serves as the residence for a high-ranking Coast Guard officer.

HOW TO GET THERE:

The lighthouse is located in Tawas Point State Park. To reach the lighthouse, drive about 1½ miles west of Tawas City on U.S. 23, then turn right onto Tawas Beach Road. Continue into the park and drive to the beach parking area at the end of the road. Follow the walking path to the lighthouse, which can be seen from the parking area. The tower is open to the public in June, and the Coast Guard offers tours during most summer months. For information on tours call (517) 362–4429. Camping facilities and picnic tables are available in the park.

A fourth-order Fresnel lens lights up the lantern room atop Tawas Point Lighthouse.

STURGEON POINT LIGHT

Alcona, Michigan – 1870

Beaming from the top of a sixty-eight-foot light tower, Sturgeon Point Lighthouse has saved many lives since it was placed in service in 1870. Today the light continues to guide mariners and warn them away from a nearby ship-killing reef. Although the light station remains active, nowadays it serves as a museum. Occasionally, visitors can climb the eighty-five steps of the tower's cast-iron stairway.

Standing beside the 3.5-order lens inside the lantern room and gazing out across the lake, one is reminded of the life-or-death dramas that have taken place in this dangerous stretch of water.

On August 27, 1880, the wooden steamer *Marine City* took on a cargo of shingles at Alcona. Along with the shingles came three Detroit-bound stowaways, who apparently had concealed themselves in the cargo hold. Their passage would not be free, however. In fact, they would pay dearly for it. For two hours the *Marine City* made good time in a freshening breeze that kicked up white-capped waves on the lake. Then calamity struck. Smoke and flames were seen coming from the hurricane deck, near its juncture with the ship's funnel. Passengers rushed to either side of the ship's weather deck as flames began to engulf the tinderbox superstructure.

A pair of tugboats were the first rescue vessels at the scene. When her captain saw the smoke, the tugboat *Vulcan* steamed at top speed toward the *Marine City*. Just exiting the Black River, the tugboat *Grayling* cut loose the barge she was towing and set out in the wake of the *Vulcan*. The Sturgeon Point Lifesaving crew, as well as John Pasque, the lighthouse keeper, joined in the rescue effort. Of 121 passengers and crew aboard the *Marine City,* all but twenty were rescued. Among those thought to have died in the flames were the three stowaways.

There have been many disasters and near-disasters in the vicinity of Sturgeon Point. In October 1887 the 233-ton schooner *Venus,* loaded with grindstones, foundered off Black River, with the loss of seven lives. In 1903 the crew of the three-masted schooner *Ispeming* were forced to abandon ship. Fortunately, all were rescued by a tug.

A tragedy unseen except by those who perished occurred in September 1924, when the vessel *Clifton,* loaded with stone, disappeared during a fierce gale that swept Lake Huron. The last recorded sighting of the *Clifton* was at 7:00 A.M. on the same day that the vessel cleared Old Mackinac Point. Following the storm, wreckage was found off Black River, forty-five miles southeast of Alpena. Among the debris were an empty raft and a pilothouse clock, which had stopped at 4:00 P.M.

Automated in 1936, the Sturgeon Point Light Station was purchased and renovated by the Alcona County Historical Society. The keeper's quarters houses museum exhibits. On display on the grounds outside is the big rudder salvaged from the *Marine City.*

HOW TO GET THERE:

The museum in the keeper's house is open daily from Memorial Day to Labor Day. During the fall color season, the museum is open weekends. For exact hours and other information, call (517) 724–6297. To reach the lighthouse, take U.S. 23 North from Harrisville, then turn right onto Point Road. The parking lot for the lighthouse is located less than a mile down the road.

LIGHTS OF PRESQUE ISLE

Old Presque Isle Light – 1840

New Presque Isle Light – 1871

Built in 1870 on a peninsula jutting into Lake Huron and still guiding vessels to this day, the New Presque Isle Light beams from one of the highest towers on the Great Lakes. Now automated, the light was authorized in the 1860s by President Abraham Lincoln. Its beacon is visible for twenty-five miles and is used as a bearing by commercial vessels bound for Lakes Michigan and Superior.

The 113-foot light tower and the attached rectangular brick keeper's house are the centerpiece for a 100-acre public park maintained by Presque Isle Township. The park also includes Old Presque Isle Lighthouse, which was completed in 1840 and discontinued in 1871, when the new tower took over its duties. There are also range lights, which were used to mark the harbor channel. These venerable structures occupy a cedar- and pine-covered peninsula that helps form Presque Isle Harbor on one side and North Bay on the other side.

The need for a lighthouse on the peninsula was recognized during the early 1830s, when an increasing number of commercial vessels began using Presque Isle Harbor for shelter as well as for a source of cordwood to fire their boilers. After Congress appropriated $5,000 to build a light station, the contract for the thirty-foot-high, stone-and-brick light tower and a keeper's cottage was awarded to Jeremiah Moors of Detroit, who completed the work in September 1840. The first keeper was Henry L. Woolsey, who held the job until replaced by Patrick Garrity some twenty-one years afterward, at the beginning of the Civil War.

In March 1869 Congress appropriated $7,500 to construct range lights on shore to mark the channel for vessels bound in and out of the harbor. The front range light was housed in a fifteen-foot-high, octagonal wood-frame structure. The rear light was located about 800 feet away and thirty-six feet above lake level. Both range lights have been discontinued. The rear range lighthouse is now a private residence.

New Presque Isle Light and its cottage were completed in 1871. Garrity and his wife, Anna, happily moved from the old keeper's dwelling

The New Presque Isle Lighthouse soars 113 feet above its placid surroundings. The attached dwelling suggests a farmhouse.

to the more spacious new one. The gable-roofed house was connected to the tower by an enclosed walkway. During their tenure at the two stations, the Garritys reared ten children. Anna Garrity is said to have maintained nightlong vigils looking out over the lake from a rocking chair at the rear range light.

The tower base is nineteen feet, three inches tall and is capped with an iron watchroom and a ten-sided cast-iron lantern, which still contains its original third-order Fresnel lens crafted by Henry LaPaute of Paris. In the late 1980s the tower was restored to its original condition. Extensive work has also been done to the keeper's cottage. Both are open seasonally to the public.

In 1885 Thomas Garrity took over from his father and was keeper of New Presque Isle Light until 1935, a remarkable fifty-year tenure. Coastguardsmen occupied the station from 1939 until the early 1970s, when the light was automated and the keeper's house boarded up.

There is a persistent story about a lighthouse ghost, said to be that of a keeper's wife (not Mrs. Garrity) driven insane by the isolation. Supposedly, she was locked up permanently by her husband. Some say that, on windy nights, you can hear the screams of a woman coming from inside one of the lighthouses (it's not clear which).

Old Presque Isle Lighthouse is said by some to be haunted.

HOW TO GET THERE:

From Presque Isle, follow Grand Lake Road past the intersection of Highway 638, or from U.S. 23, take Highway 638 to Grand Lake Road and turn left. A little more than ½ mile to the north are the Old Presque Isle Lighthouse and Museum. A pair of range light towers stands nearby. From the museum continue north about 1 mile on Grand Lake Road to New Presque Isle Lighthouse, which is surrounded by a scenic 100-acre park. There are also a fine museum and gift shop here. The four lighthouses (old and new, front and rear range) offer the visitor an especially valuable lesson in lighthouse history and lore.

Spiral steps climb toward the lantern room at Old Presque Isle Lighthouse.

FORTY MILE POINT LIGHT

Rogers City, Michigan – 1897

Until the late 1890s the fifty-mile stretch of shoreline between Cheboygan and Presque Isle Lighthouse was dark and threatening to mariners. Here was a dangerous gap in an otherwise almost unbroken chain of navigational lights guiding ships through the Great Lakes. In 1894 Congress decided to fill the gap and appropriated $25,000 to build a light station at Forty Mile Point.

Completed in 1896 and placed in operation the following year, the square brick tower stands fifty-three feet tall. At the top an octagonal, black-trimmed cast-iron lantern contains a fourth-order Fresnel lens displaying a flashing white light. Painted white, the tower stands in sharp contrast to the attached natural-brick keeper's dwelling.

The architecture of the two-story dwelling is quite interesting and features a pair of gables, one gable on either side of the tower. The station also has a well-preserved brick oil house and fog-signal building.

Down on the beach below the lighthouse is the rotting hulk of a wooden ship wrecked here in the distant past. Visitors often walk the beach looking for puddingstones (the remnants of a volcanic eruption many millions of years ago).

HOW TO GET THERE:

The well-maintained tower, dwelling, and other structures are not open to the public at this time, but the grounds and buildings are quite beautiful and well worth a visit. About 6 miles north of Rogers City on U.S. 23, you will encounter a sign directing you to Presque Isle County Lighthouse Park. Turn right onto an otherwise unmarked road and follow it to the lighthouse (do not take Forty Mile Point Road).

As ships approach the Straits of Mackinac from the Lake Huron side, they enter one of the most dangerous stretches of water in the Great Lakes region—or perhaps anywhere. Here the broad waters of Lake Huron narrow down to just a few miles in width, and ships squeezing through this area must run an obstacle course of treacherous shallows and ship-killing reefs.

Among the most deadly of these is Spectacle Reef (above, courtesy U.S. Coast Guard), a pair of clawlike shoals lurking a few feet below sea level. The loss of two large schooners here in 1867 spurred demands from sailors and shipping interests that something be done to mark these vicious shoals. Soon afterward Congress appropriated $100,000 to build a lighthouse directly over the shoals. Though a princely sum for the time, the appropriation would prove inadequate.

Two lighthouse tenders and more than 200 men worked for nearly four years to complete the project. When it was finally finished, in 1874, it had cost taxpayers some $406,000. More than 120 years later, its (now solar-powered) light still serves lake sailors. The tower contains the original second-order Fresnel lens. The government eventually built lighthouses on several other dangerous shoals near the straits, among them Round Island, Poe Reef, and DeTour Point. All of the lighthouses contain their original Fresnel lenses, and all have been automated.

OLD MACKINAC POINT LIGHT

Mackinaw City, Michigan – 1892

When the bridge over the Mackinac Straits opened in 1957, Old Mackinac Point Light became obsolete. Vessels that once took bearings from the forty-foot-tall, turn-of-the-century light began ranging on the bridge's lights instead. In 1960 the lighthouse was converted into a maritime museum, as part of a twenty-seven-acre historical park operated by the Mackinac Island State Park Commission.

The light at Mackinaw City, which guided vessels through the straits connecting Lake Michigan and Lake Huron, evolved from a fog-signal station that first went into operation in November 1890. During one especially foggy stretch in its second year of operation, the fog signal was run for 327 hours, the boilers consuming fifty-two cords of wood.

In the late nineteenth century, Great Lakes shipping rapidly increased in volume. Vessels got bigger and technology more sophisticated. The existing Mackinac Straits sentinels at McGulpin's Point and St. Helena's Island were considered inadequate, under certain circumstances, for vessels approaching from the west. The

need for a light at Old Mackinac Point became apparent almost as soon as the fog signal was completed.

On March 3, 1891, Congress appropriated $20,000 to build a lighthouse. The buff-colored brick tower and attached keeper's dwelling were completed on October 27, 1892. The fourth-order lens light atop the tower had gone into service on the night of October 25, 1892.

About the same time that the lighthouse was built, federal officials decided to move the fog signal. The new site for the signal intruded into a park recently established by Mackinaw City. Unable to persuade the villagers to give up their park, federal authorities condemned the land. The village fought the condemnation, creating a legal snarl not resolved until 1905, when the federal government agreed to pay Mackinaw City $400 for the land. In 1906 the fog-signal building was finally moved to its new site and was later replaced by a brick building. By the mid-twentieth century, a 132-foot-high radio-beacon tower was erected beside the old brick fog-signal building.

A colorful roof gives the Old Mackinac Point Lighthouse a festive appearance. This light once marked the heavily trafficked Straits of Mackinac, which connect Lakes Michigan and Huron. Today the building houses a maritime museum.

The lights of Mackinac Bridge, shown here reaching into the distance, now mark the straits for shipping. Once the bridge opened in 1957, the nearby lighthouse was no longer needed.

HOW TO GET THERE:

From exit 336 off I–75, follow Nicolet Avenue through Mackinaw City, then turn right onto Huron Avenue. About 2 blocks down is the parking area for the Old Mackinac Point Lighthouse. The area around the lighthouse is a lovely park, with plenty of picnic tables and a wonderful view of the Mackinac Bridge. The nearby Riviera on the Beach Motel provides a romantic spot for an overnight stay and leisurely enjoyment of the lighthouse and bridge.

Its flags flying in a breeze blowing in off Lake Huron, Goderich Main Lighthouse puts on a colorful display. The bright red lantern room stands atop a squared-off, thirty-five-foot masonry tower. An iron railing protects the gallery, or walkway, which is used for exterior maintenance and cleaning the lantern windows. The light blue banner is the Goderich town flag.

CHAPTER FOUR

Lights of
THE IMPERIAL COAST
THE CANADIAN SHORES

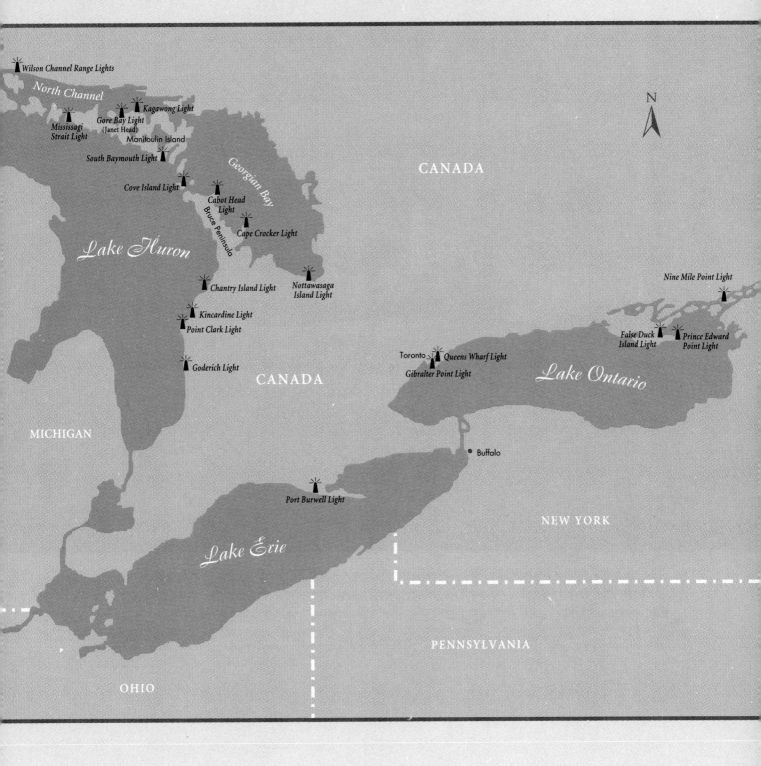

Wilson Channel Range Lights

North Channel

Kagawong Light

Gore Bay Light
(Janet Head)

Mississagi
Strait Light

Manitoulin Island

South Baymouth Light

CANADA

Georgian Bay

Cove Island Light

Cabot Head
Light

Bruce Peninsula

Cape Crocker Light

Lake Huron

N

Nine Mile Point Light

Chantry Island Light

Nottawasaga
Island Light

Kincardine Light

Point Clark Light

False Duck
Island Light

Prince Edward
Point Light

Goderich Light

CANADA

Toronto

Queens Wharf Light

Gibralter Point Light

Lake Ontario

MICHIGAN

Buffalo

NEW YORK

Port Burwell Light

Lake Erie

PENNSYLVANIA

OHIO

One of Canada's fine Imperial Towers, Nottawasaga Island Lighthouse stands its lonely vigil several miles from the Ontario mainland. Without its light, the small island would be a constant threat to vessels. Populated only by ducks, gulls, and other feathered residents, Nottawasaga Island is a bird sanctuary.

Since they serve all ships and sailors without regard to nationality, lighthouses are a country's best ambassadors. This is particularly true of lighthouses on the Great Lakes, where they not only make navigation easier and safer but also provide a highly visible link of friendship between the United States and Canada.

Together with the St. Lawrence River, the Great Lakes form one of the most extensive watery borders in the world—and one of the most peaceful. The United States and Canada have not taken up arms against one another in more than 180 years. This friendly relationship between the two nations is partly due to a common heritage but also to the need for efficient management of the lakes as a natural resource and commercial thoroughfare.

BRIDGES *of* LIGHT *and* WATER

In almost every sense, the United States and Canada share the Great Lakes. The St. Lawrence Seaway, which opened the interior of the continent to oceangoing freighters and enriched both countries, was a joint venture. To reach the bustling freshwater ports of Toronto, Cleveland, Detroit, Chicago, and Thunder Bay, ships moving up the seaway from the Atlantic must pass in and out of American and Canadian jurisdiction many times. The crews of these ships are often unsure whether they are in U.S. or Canadian waters. The Welland Canal is Canadian; the Soo Locks, American and Canadian. Only Michigan is an all-American lake, and Canadian vessels ply its waters everyday during the shipping season. In other words, instead of separating the two countries, the lakes help bring them together.

The international quality of the lakes comes into clearest focus when their restless waters turn violent. The captain of a freighter caught in a storm on the lakes does not care whether his ship is on the Canadian or American side—only that it remains afloat. The crew of a foundering vessel is equally joyous at the sight of either a Canadian Coast Guard or U.S. Coast Guard cutter. Shipwrecked sailors don't much care about the nationality of their rescuers.

To help keep wrecks to the minimum and guide vessels safely to their destination, a continuous line of lighthouses marks both sides of the seaway, from the mouth of the St. Lawrence River all the way to the far end of Lake Superior, a shoreline distance of more than a thousand miles. Those lighthouses on the Canadian side are in every way as varied, historical, and beautiful as their counterparts on the opposite shores. This chapter offers a sampling of some of the finest Canadian lighthouses on the eastern Great Lakes.

THE SAGA *of the* HAMONIC

No matter how powerful their beacons, lighthouses cannot save every ship in trouble. Occasionally, even the modern era, with all its electronic wizardry, calamity strikes on the Great Lakes. Consider the tragic loss of the *Edmund Fitzgerald,* the 729-foot ore freighter that disappeared with all her crew in a November gale in 1975.

Some Great Lakes shipping disasters, however, are not so much tragic as they are ironic. One such incident was the destruction of the passenger liner *Hamonic* while she was tied to the dock in her home port in Ontario.

Built in 1909 at the shipyards in Collingwood, Ontario, the *Hamonic* was a princess of a ship, with its wide decks, comfortable staterooms, and luxurious fittings. Like her sister ship, the *Noronic* (see page 68), she was much loved by her faithful crew and by passengers, some of whom sailed on her regularly for more than thirty years.

The *Hamonic* came very near to ending her career after only a few seasons of service. When the mighty storm of November 1913 struck the Midwest, most other passenger ships had retired from the lakes for the winter. But the storm's hurricane-force winds caught the *Hamonic* plowing northward through Lake Superior on her last run of the year. Towering waves smashed pilothouse windows, ripped cables and railings from the deck, and forced the ship to run for the cover of Whitefish Bay.

The lighthouse on Whitefish Point helped guide the beleaguered vessel to the calmer waters of the bay, but by this time the ship had taken on so much water that she was in danger of sinking. To save her, the captain ran her aground near the shore. Incredibly, no one was killed or seriously injured, and after the storm, the crew managed to refloat the *Hamonic* and steam back to her home port at Sarnia, Ontario, on Lake Huron.

Twelve years later, another November storm caught the *Hamonic* once more exposed, this time on the open, unforgiving waters of Lake Superior. The ship lost a propeller and, wallowing in the heavy seas, almost rolled over and sank. The *Richard Trimble,* an enormous American freighter hurrying south to escape the worst of the storm, caught sight of the *Hamonic.* After standing by the stricken ship all night, the *Trimble* managed to take her in tow and shepherd her to safety.

The *Hamonic* had many other adventures on the lakes; but the strangest, and certainly the most fateful, came on July 17, 1945, near the end of World War II. Early that morning the passenger liner had steamed up the St. Clair River, slipped into the harbor at Sarnia, and docked near Point Edward. The berths of the thirty-six-year-old ship were still filled with sleeping passengers. Also sleeping soundly was Captain Horace Beaton, who had commanded the *Hamonic* for many years.

Then it happened. In a huge warehouse beside the dock, a piece of loading machinery overheated and caught fire. Fanned by a strong breeze, the flames quickly spread to packing crates, pallets, cartons, and the wooden walls of the warehouse itself. Within minutes the breeze had made a block-long blowtorch of the building and trained its intense heat directly onto the *Hamonic.* The ship's steel hull grew red-hot, and flames shot up from the dockside decks.

Awakened by the commotion, Captain Beaton hurried to the pilothouse. There he confronted a situation more desperate than any he had faced in all his years of fighting through gale-force winds and mountainous waves out on the lakes. Although the weather was good and the *Hamonic* was tied securely to the dock in the seeming safety of her home port, the bright orange flames rolling up over decks made it all too apparent that Beaton was now the captain of a doomed ship. But he had no time to consider the irony; he had to act quickly or not at all.

The fire had consumed the wooden dock, and a wall of flame blocked access to the entire port side of the ship. Everyone on board the *Hamonic*—all its hundreds of passengers and crew—were trapped! The captain had to try to get the *Hamonic* away from the blazing warehouse. Beaton gave the order to cast off lines, and he rang for steam. He could only hope that someone was still on duty in the engine room, which he imagined by this time had become an inferno.

Aware of the crisis, Chief Engineer James Neilson was down in the bowels of the ship, struggling to raise steam in the boilers. The fire had reached the storage lockers just above the engine room, and exploding jars and cans showered Neilson with steaming pickle juice and hot vegetables. But somehow he managed to get just enough power to the ship's engines to allow Captain Beaton to back the burning vessel away from the dock.

This would be the most important cruise of the *Hamonic*'s career. It would also be her shortest. After moving only a few hundred yards, she ran aground beside a construction area near the docks. The *Hamonic* had now become no less an inferno than the warehouse itself, and Beaton set about the task of rescuing passengers. He got some very welcome help from the shore, where a quick-thinking construction worker cranked up his steam shovel and started lifting passengers off the deck with its big scoop. Other passengers and crew jumped overboard. Some were plucked from the water by the captain himself, who brought a small boat around to the ship's starboard side. The last person that Beaton rescued was Chief Engineer Neilson, who, just short of being broiled alive, dove into the water through a ring of flame.

Eventually, everyone was safely brought ashore. Miraculously, the disaster had produced not a single fatality; but, not so fortunate as her passengers and crew, the *Hamonic* continued to burn throughout the day. She was a goner. A few weeks later she would be towed to her final, inglorious resting place, a scrapyard in Detroit.

This photograph makes the Prince Edward Point Lighthouse look as if it is ready for duty, but not so. The lantern shown here actually belongs to a nearby steel skeleton tower. Built in 1881, the old lighthouse served until it was replaced by its steel neighbor in 1959. Later, the lantern room was removed from the old lighthouse. As the red barn in the foreground suggests, the land around the light station was used for agricultural purposes.

NINE MILE POINT LIGHT

Simcoe Island, Ontario – 1834

The long finger of Simcoe Island thrusts south-westward into Lake Ontario as if to point the way to Toronto, St. Catherines, the Welland Canal, and Lake Erie and thence onward to Lakes Huron, Michigan, and Superior. Countless thousands of ships have followed this liquid highway deep into the heart of the North American continent. And for more than 160 years, the captains of vessels sailing out of the St. Lawrence River and onto Lake Ontario have been able to look over their shoulders and see a light winking at them from Nine Mile Point, on the lakeward tip of Simcoe Island.

The Nine Mile Point Lighthouse was the first link in a chain of lights stretching hundreds of miles from Kingston, at the eastern end of Lake Ontario, to Thunder Bay, near the far end of Lake Superior. This light once was thought to be of vital strategic importance. The government of Upper Canada considered construction of a lighthouse here a priority, and in 1833 it provided 750 pounds sterling ($2,918) for the purpose. But these were far more frugal times than our own, and apparently not all of this money was spent. A patriotic island property owner donated land for the station, on the condition that the government "put up a good fence." The station's iron lantern was purchased for 139 pounds ($542), while another 172 pounds ($670) went to provide lamps, reflectors, oil burners, and other supplies. Construction of the tower—often the most expensive single consideration when establishing a light station—cost about 317 pounds ($1,236). The forty-five-foot stone structure, built by one Robert Mathews, proved to have been worth every shilling. The tower still stands today, despite more than one and a half centuries of buffeting by storm-driven winds whistling off the lake.

The original lighting apparatus included three reflectors that produced synchronized flashes as they revolved around a central lamp. A clockwork mechanism, driven by weighted cables dropping down the center of the tower, kept the reflectors in motion. Keepers got little sleep at night, since they had to hand-crank the weight back to top of the tower every three hours.

Less worrisome for the keepers was the 1,000-pound fog bell, installed here in 1874. In fog or foul weather, a gear-driven hammer struck the bell to warn sailors away from the island. Interestingly, the bell and striker machinery cost 327 pounds ($1,273)—more than Mathews had been paid to build the station's tower. The bell was eventually replaced by an automated horn. The Canadian Coast Guard discontinued the fog signal in 1991.

HOW TO GET THERE:

"Getting there is half the fun." This adage was never half so true as when used to describe a visit to Nine Mile Point Lighthouse. If you are up for adventure, take Canadian Highway 2 or I–401 (the Cartier Freeway) to the charming town of Kingston. Ontario Street leads to the Wolfe Island Ferry Dock. There you can take advantage of a rare traveler's bargain: a free ferry ride across the fabled St. Lawrence River. Once on Wolfe Island, go straight ahead on Center Street and turn right onto Highway 96. After 3.5 miles you'll see a gravel road on the right. It leads to an old-fashioned, cable-driven ferry—there's a small toll—which will take you to Simcoe Island. The island's only road ends at the lighthouse. Once back in Kingston, you'll want to visit the Marine Museum of the Great Lakes. Located on the Kingston waterfront, the museum is open from 10:00 A.M. to 5:00 P.M. every day except Christmas. Nearby is the Alexander Henry, a decommissioned Canadian ice breaker, now used as a bed and breakfast. Also in the area is the Pumphouse, a unique industrial museum devoted to steam power. For information on the museums or B&B, call (613) 542–2261.

LIGHTS OF PRINCE EDWARD COUNTY

False Duck Island – 1829

Prince Edward Point – 1881

Prince Edward County juts into Lake Ontario like a Swiss Army knife with all its utility blades extended. The county's jagged peninsulas and rocky landfalls have torn open the bellies of many fine vessels and remain to this day an ever-present threat to shipping in some of the most heavily trafficked waters on the planet. The depths near the county shoreline are known collectively to locals and mariners alike as a "graveyard of ships."

To save lives and encourage commerce, the Canadian government began marking the most prominent obstacles with lights during the early 1800s. The building and rebuilding of light stations here continued for more than a century, and as a consequence, the county became home to one of the most varied assortments of lighthouses ever seen on the North American continent.

At one time or another, at least twelve separate light stations have guarded the county's shores: the lighthouses at False Duck Island (built in 1829), Point Petre (1833), Presqu'ile Point (1854), Scotch Bonnet Reef (1856), Point Pleasant (1866), Telegraph Island (1870), Salmon Point (1871), Point Traverse (1881), Prince Edward Point (1881), Makatewis Island (1894), Onderdonk Point (1911), and Main Duck Island (1913). But time has been as hard on these old lighthouses as the county itself has been on ships. All but a few of the lighthouses have been abandoned, and most have fallen into ruins or disappeared altogether.

The oldest lighthouse in the county stood for many years on False Duck Island, which, as you might guess, was often mistaken by ships' pilots for Main Duck Island. Built of concrete and stone at a cost of approximately 1,000 British pounds ($3,890), the station featured a sixty-three-foot tower displaying a fixed white light provided by oil lamps.

One night in 1905 an extraordinarily powerful trident of lightning struck the station, blasting apart the lantern room and burning the dwelling and oil house to the ground. Keeper Dorland Dulmage and his family survived the calamity and spent the night shivering in the foghorn building, the only structure on the island not hit by lightning.

The station was fully restored and served until 1965, when the venerable lighthouse was replaced by an automated navigational marker.

This seaman's memorial is crowned by the lantern and lens from the old False Duck Island Lighthouse.

Now all but forgotten, the Prince Edward Island Lighthouse lost its lantern room after it was replaced by the adjacent metal tower.

That same year a Canadian Coast Guard tender hooked a cable to the historic tower and pulled it to ground, thus accomplishing what lightning had not: the utter destruction of a national treasure. The lantern and lighting mechanism were salvaged from the ruins and placed on top of a thirty-foot limestone tower in Mariner's Memorial Park on Quinte Isle. Built in 1967, the tower honors the many seamen who have lost their lives on Lake Ontario.

Only a few miles from the park stands a memorial of a different sort: the decaying remains of Prince Edward Point Lighthouse. Built in 1881, it guided mariners for almost eighty years before finally giving up its job to a fully automated light atop a nearby steel-skeleton tower. When it was decommissioned in 1959, the old lighthouse suffered the indignity of having its lantern removed, and it has been more or less neglected ever since. Indeed, nowadays paint peels from the tapered wooden walls of the decapitated tower.

Not all of the county's light stations serve only as memorials, however. After more than eighty years of nightly vigilance, the Main Duck Island Lighthouse still flashes its warning to ships every six seconds. Established shortly before World War I, the station marks the western end of Main Duck Island, a fifteen-mile-long barrier of ship-killing rock more than a dozen miles from the Ontario mainland. The seventy-foot octagonal tower contains a rotating, third-order Fresnel lens, producing an intermittent beam visible from sixteen miles away.

HOW TO GET THERE:

From the town of Picton on Highway 33, drive south to Cherry Valley. Following County Road 10, go 5 miles to Milford and then take County Road 9 about 3 miles to Mariner's Memorial Park. The museum here features excellent nautical exhibits and a fine collection of old-time sailing artifacts. The museum is open from 10:00 A.M. to 5:00 P.M. every day during July and August and on weekends only during June, September, October, and November.

For Prince Edward Point Lighthouse, continue from Memorial Park on County Road 9 for an additional 13 miles. The road will turn to gravel about ½ mile from the lighthouse.

Main Duck Island Lighthouse can be reached from the mainland only by boat and, being a federal facility, is off-limits to the public.

LIGHTS OF TORONTO

Gibraltar Point Light – 1806

Queen's Wharf Light – 1861

The foremost mission of a lighthouse is to save ships and the lives of those on board. Marine disasters, however, all too often strike when a vessel is beyond the assistance of any light or other navigational aid. The strong hand of fate may take control of events when a ship is far from shore or even, as in the following case, when she is tethered to the seeming safety of a dock.

On the afternoon of September 16, 1949, the passenger steamer *Noronic* eased into her berth in Toronto

after an uneventful trip from Cleveland via Lakes Erie and Ontario and the Welland Canal. Having served vacationers and other lake travelers for more than thirty-six years, the *Noronic* was nearing retirement. Even so, she was a comfortable and dependable ship, and those who frequented her spacious decks knew her affectionately as the *Norrie*.

It was late Friday afternoon when the ship came into port in Toronto, and many of the 695 passengers and crew hurried ashore to enjoy an evening in the big city. By midnight most were back on board and asleep in their cabins. Shortly after one o'clock on Saturday morning, a passenger strolling along a corridor noticed smoke curling from a sealed locker. With the help of a passing bellboy, he forced open the locker. Inside was a seething mass of flame that seemed to reach far down into the ship. The two separated and ran off to give the alarm, but wherever they went throughout the ship, long tongues of flame licked close behind. For many of the soundly sleeping passengers, the alarm would come too late. Trapped by a wall of fire or overcome by smoke, 118 of them would be dead before the night was over, making this one of the worst shipping disasters in Great Lakes' history.

Ironically, this calamity took place within a few steps of dry land. And if they had looked out toward the lake, passengers and crew of the doomed *Noronic* might have seen the glow of the Gibraltar Point Lighthouse, though the light could offer them no guidance or comfort now. In fact, their own vessel had become a gruesome sort of lighthouse, a huge torch visible to everyone in Toronto and to sailors far out on Lake Ontario.

The Toronto Fire Department responded quickly and fought the blaze from the dock. Except for the magnitude of the blaze, this might have been an ordinary hotel fire. But no matter how much water the firemen poured on the ship, the flames only seemed to leap higher. Eventually, the *Noronic* sank under the

Built in 1806, the Gibraltar Point Lighthouse is a well-known Toronto landmark. Some say it is haunted by the ghost of a former keeper who was murdered here in 1815.

weight of the water from the hoses, and only then did the fire surrender to the cold lake.

To this day no one knows exactly where the fire began or why it spread so quickly. The answers to these mysteries were likely obliterated, along with the gutted *Noronic*, when, a few weeks after the fire, she was sliced up by salvagers and sold as scrap steel.

While the Gibraltar Point Lighthouse could do nothing to assist the *Noronic*, it has saved hundreds, perhaps thousands, of vessels by guiding them to safety. A lighthouse does its most effective lifesaving work when a disaster does *not* occur. Who can say how many wrecks there might have been if not for the tall octagonal tower on Gibraltar Point? One of the earliest navigational markers on the Great Lakes, the lighthouse was built in 1806 on the lakeward crook of a low, sandy island shaped like a fishhook. The brown-brick tower served mariners for more than 150 years before being replaced by a fully automated light mounted on a simple iron tower in 1958.

Gibraltar Point is said to be haunted. The very first keeper of the lighthouse here was a man named Rademuller. In 1815 Rademuller vanished from the island and was never seen or heard from again. Some years later, however, his skeleton was unearthed near the tower, making it apparent that the hapless keeper had been murdered. His ghost is said to walk the island

and to climb the lighthouse steps at night. Perhaps he is joined by phantoms from the *Noronic*.

Back on the mainland, in a park just off Toronto's busy Fleet Street, stands one of Canada's most interesting and unique lighthouses. The Queen's Wharf Lighthouse was one of a pair of range lights that once marked the safe channel into the Toronto harbor. Established in 1861, these lights served until 1912, when the opening of a new harbor entrance made them unnecessary. One of the wooden towers was torn down, but the other survived. In 1929, after years of neglect, the remaining lighthouse was patched up, given a fresh coat of red paint, and trucked off to a new career as the centerpiece of a city park. The enclosed metal lantern and protruding lenses make it look like the head of a metal monster in a bad science fiction movie. Perhaps this is why the little lighthouse is so popular among children.

HOW TO GET THERE:

To reach Gibraltar Point Lighthouse, start at the Island Ferries Terminal, just off Queen's Quay and Young Street on the Toronto waterfront. Take the ferry to Harlan Point, where you can bike, take a shuttle, or hike about a mile to the lighthouse. (This is an excellent destination for a day hike.) For information on ferry and shuttle schedules, call (416) 392–8186. Some harbor cruises available at the waterfront pass by Gibraltar Point, offering an excellent opportunity for photography.

The Queen's Wharf Lighthouse is located off Fleet Street, not far from Exhibition Stadium. To find it and other key Toronto attractions, use of a good city map is recommended.

After a half century of guiding ships in and out of Toronto Harbor, the Queens Wharf Lighthouse now serves as centerpiece of a small city park.

PORT BURWELL LIGHT

Port Burwell, Ontario – 1840

One of the most beautiful wooden structures in all Canada, the classic octagonal tower of the Port Burwell Lighthouse has stood since 1840. The tower's gently sloping walls are sixty-five feet high and crested by a small, eight-sided lantern room containing a fourth-order Fresnel lens.

The Canadian Coast Guard decommissioned the light in 1963, after 123 years of service. Astonishingly, for all but the first twelve of those years, the lighthouse was looked after by members of the same family. Alexander Sutherland became keeper in 1852. He was succeeded in the post by his sons and grandsons right up until the light was finally extinguished, a family service record of 111 years in all.

Although the lighthouse no longer guides ships, a ceremonial light still burns atop the tower. The old lighthouse is carefully maintained by citizens of Port Burwell, who consider it a vital link to their past. Using traditional hand tools, Mennonite craftsmen completed renovations in 1986. Near the lighthouse is the Port Burwell Marine Museum, which contains a fine collection of lighthouse and maritime artifacts. Especially noteworthy among the displays is the three-sided bull's-eye lens and rotation drive that once served at the nearby Old Long Point Lighthouse.

HOW TO GET THERE:

From Highway 3, just south of the town of Tillsonburg, turn south on Highway 19 and follow it through Eden, Straffordville, and Vienna to Port Burwell. Here Highway 19 becomes Erieus Street and then Robinson Street, which ends near the lighthouse. Both the lighthouse and museum are open to the public daily during the summer months and at all other times by appointment. For information or to make an appointment call (519) 874–4204 or (519) 874–4343.

Using only traditional hand tools, Mennonite craftsmen restored the Port Burwell Lighthouse in 1986. Today, it stands as a handsome reminder of a bygone era.

LIGHTS OF MANITOULIN ISLAND

Mississagi Straits Light – 1873

Janet Head Light – 1879

Kagawong Light – 1880 and 1888

South Baymouth Range Light – 1898

Between the open expanses of Lake Huron and the blue-green waters of Georgian Bay sits mammoth Manitoulin Island. Roughly fifty times the size of New York's Manhattan Island, it encompasses 1,068 square miles, making it the largest island in the Great Lakes. In fact, it is the largest island in any lake in the world.

Of course, size is not the only thing distinguishing Manitoulin from Manhattan. Instead of a monument to concrete, steel, and urbanity, Manitoulin Island is a paradise of forests, farms, and picturesque villages. But there are bright lights here, too.

A wave-washed rock the size of Manitoulin has to be well marked with lighthouses, and the Canadian government began to establish light stations here as early as the 1850s. More than a dozen key light towers once guarded the island's shores, and many of these still stand.

Built in 1873, the oldest surviving lighthouse on the island still maintains its vigil beside the crucial Mississagi Straits. The light, mounted atop a square, forty-foot wooden tower, once guided ships passing between the broad North Channel and Lake Huron. Although the lighthouse was taken out of service in 1970, a nearby automated light continues its vitally important work.

The tower rises from a corner of a modest dwelling where keepers once lived with their families. For these keepers, the Mississagi Straits Lighthouse was a particularly isolated duty station. The only way in or out was over a rugged trail or by boat; not until 1968, when the light was about to be automated, did construction crews push through a road to the station. Nevertheless, the longevity of service for keepers at this station was remarkable. During almost a century of operation, only five different keepers served here. W. A. Grant kept the light for almost thirty-three years, living at this remote outpost with his wife and family from 1913 until 1946. A local historical society operates a museum here during the summer and has filled the dwelling with authentic period furnishings. It is easy to imagine that any of the station's keepers could step into the dwelling and feel right at home.

Not far from the lighthouse are the remains of a

Although modest in appearance, the Mississagi Straits Lighthouse marks a vital passage between the North Channel and Lake Huron. (Courtesy Helen Van Every)

Now a private residence, the Janet Head Lighthouse has a warm, homey look.

very old shipwreck, believed by some to be that of the *Griffin*, the first European ship to sail the Great Lakes. Launched by the early French explorer Sieur de La Salle, the *Griffin* disappeared mysteriously in 1679 (see page 1).

Very similar to the Mississagi Straits Lighthouse is the twenty-five-foot tower and attached dwelling at Janet Head. During the 1820s a British naval officer named this headland for his daughter. Built in 1879, the Janet Head Lighthouse was retired in 1940. This station also had five different keepers, the longest term of service being that of Robert Lewis who kept the light from 1913 until 1932.

To mark the harbor of the industrious village of Kagawong, the Canadian government established a light on Mudge Bay in 1880. It shined from a small tower built out over the water at the end of a dock. A fire, probably sparked by the coal-oil lamps in the lantern room, soon destroyed the tower, and it was replaced by a small pyramidal structure built on shore. Completed in 1888, Kagawong's second lighthouse survives to this day. The thirty-foot wooden tower supports a square lantern room displaying a red light visible from thirteen miles away.

A slightly taller pyramidal tower still marks the western shore of Manitowaning Bay, just as it has since 1885. The thirty-five-foot-tall lighthouse stands on a hill in the village of Manitowaning. Beaming from an octagonal lantern room, its green light can be seen from a distance of up to sixteen miles.

At South Baymouth, near the entrance to whale-shaped South Bay, a Tweedledee–Tweedledum range lighthouse combination teams up to mark the safe channel for vessels approaching the town. Built in 1898, the white wooden towers stand about 250 yards apart; they are so similar in appearance that looking at them in the daylight makes you wonder if you are seeing double. The structures are not identical, however. The twenty-six-foot rear tower is taller and thinner than its seventeen-foot mate located down near the water. It is the perspective that makes them look the same.

At night the structures are much more easily distinguished, because the rear tower displays a fixed white light, while the front tower displays a green light. Pilots entering the harbor try to position the white light directly above the green. Movement of the white light either to the left or right of perpendicular indicates that the vessel is straying out of the safe channel.

HOW TO GET THERE:

Manitoulin Island can be reached from the Canadian mainland on Highway 6, via the Great LaCloche Island Bridge. From the Manitoulin town of Little Current, drive approximately 20 miles along Highway 6 to Manitowaning, turn east onto Arthur Street, and follow it to the Manitowaning Lighthouse. An additional 19 miles along Highway 6 will take you to South Baymouth, with its range lights located near the marina and ferry terminal. From South Baymouth, a delightful two-hour ferry ride will take you to the Bruce Peninsula, providing a view of the Cove Island Lighthouse along the way. For ferry schedules and other information, call (705) 859–3161.

For lighthouses on the western end of Manitoulin Island, turn onto Highway 540 at Little Current and drive approximately 30 miles to Kagawong. The Kagawong Lighthouse stands beside the road just across from the town's marina. To reach Janet Head Lighthouse, go 9 miles farther on Highway 540; then turn north onto Highway 540B to the town of Gore Bay, and follow Meredith, Dawson, and Water streets to the lighthouse. Please note that the Janet Head Lighthouse is now a private residence and is closed to the public. Mississagi Lighthouse is located on the far western end of Manitoulin Island, several miles from the town of Meldrum Bay. From Highway 540, turn west onto Mississagi Lighthouse Road and drive approximately 6 miles to the light.

Only thirty feet tall, the diminutive Kagawong Lighthouse (right) has stood since 1888. The South Baymouth Front Range Lighthouse, one of a matched pair of range lights (the other is out of view on the left), guides ferries to their slip on Manitoulin Island.

LIGHTS OF THE BRUCE PENINSULA

Goderich Main Light – 1847

Kincardine Rear Range Light – 1888

Cape Crocker Light – 1898

Cabot Head Light – 1896

For anyone who loves water, Ontario's Bruce Peninsula is a destination that absolutely must be marked on the vacation calendar at least once in a lifetime, if not every year. To the east lies a sixty-mile expanse of the blue-green Georgian Bay. To the west, azure Lake Huron stretches more than a hundred miles across to the nearest land in Michigan. Barely separating these two enormous bodies of cool, freshwater, the peninsula's long, forested finger curves gently to the

northwest. Sparkling white beaches, picturesque lakeside villages, comfortable country inns, and delightful coffeehouses make the peninsula a wonderland for travelers. Compounding its charm are several of Canada's loveliest lighthouses.

Travelers headed toward the peninsula along the shore of Lake Huron will likely pass through the town of Goderich and very near one of Ontario's oldest lighthouses. On a bluff above the lake, just a few blocks off Canada's scenic Highway 21, a squarish concrete tower guards the approaches to Goderich Harbor. Only thirty-five feet tall, the Goderich Main Lighthouse is a midget compared to the Imperial Towers at Point Clark and Chantry Island to the north (see Imperial Towers, beginning on page 77). This workmanlike lighthouse does its job well, however, guiding vessels in and out of the harbor, just as it has done since 1847. Sailors seeking refuge from one of Lake Huron's furious storms may find the pudgy little structure with its powerful light more attractive than people who see it from the shore.

In Kincardine, about forty miles to the north of Goderich, stands a lighthouse that nearly everyone considers beautiful. Why shouldn't they? The unique design and picture-postcard good looks of the Kincardine Rear Range Lighthouse make film a hot-selling item for businesses in this delightful lakeshore community. The octagonal wooden tower rises gracefully some thirty feet above the roof of the dwelling. Both the tower and dwelling are painted white with red trim. Built in 1888, the lighthouse is one of two working in tandem to guide vessels into the harbor. Located on a wharf about a quarter of a mile away, the small Kincardine Front Range tower is much less remarkable.

Marking the northern shore of rectangular Colpoy's Bay, which forms a ten-mile-long slot on the east side of the Bruce Peninsula, is the Cape Crocker Lighthouse

Among Ontario's oldest and most historic navigational lights, the Goderich Main Lighthouse has served mariners since 1847.

With its striking white tower and bright red trim, the Kincardine Rear Range Lighthouse is surely one of the loveliest buildings in Canada. In the foreground pleasure craft bob in the waters of Lake Huron.

(the Imperial Tower on Griffith Island marks the southern shore). The lantern of the Cape Crocker Light is similar in style to those atop the magnificent Imperials, but the tower itself could hardly be more different. Its smooth octagonal walls are no wider than the lantern and convey the impression of a pole or pedestal. A fanciful mind might see the fifty-three-foot-tall structure as a torch designed to be carried by a giant runner—and what a torch it would be. The lantern contains a powerful, third-order Fresnel clamshell lens displaying a flashing green light.

To the northwest of Cape Crocker, squat Lion's Head Lighthouse stands forlorn and abandoned. Despite its noble name, this was never a very impressive lighthouse. The original tower stood at the end of a dock but was blown off into the bay by a storm in 1913. Set at the end of the harbor breakwater, its fifteen-foot-tall successor had more solid footing. Like the "little engine that could," it performed its duties faithfully until 1967, when it was moved to the shore and replaced by a light on a steel pole.

Located on a toe of land cleared from a tall, pristine forest, the Cape Crocker Lighthouse keeps watch over the crystal waters of Lake Huron.

The Cabot Head Lighthouse, perhaps the homiest light station on the Bruce Peninsula, appears ready for a keeper's family to move right in and live in the traditional style. The station dates to 1896. Looked after nowadays by the Friends of Cabot Head, the dwelling has been furnished with antiques and decorated in a manner reminiscent of earlier times. The group hopes to restore the tower that once rose from a corner of the dwelling. The top of the tower was lopped off several years ago when a nearby airport-style beacon went into service.

Built in 1896, the Cabot Head Lighthouse served for more than a century before losing its job in 1989 to the adjacent tower. The building is being restored to its original appearance by local citizens.

HOW TO GET THERE:

To reach *Goderich Main Lighthouse* from Highway 21 in Goderich, turn west onto East Street, go halfway around the Town Square, and continue along West Street and then Cobourg Street to the lighthouse.

For the *Kincardine Rear Range Lighthouse*, turn off Highway 21 at Kincardine Avenue and drive west approximately 1 mile to Queen Street. Follow Queen Street north for almost 1 mile, and then drive west again, on Harbour Street, for about 2 blocks. The lighthouse stands on the banks of the Penetagore River just down the hill from Harbour Street.

To reach the *Cape Crocker Lighthouse* from Highway 6 near the town of Wiarton, follow County Road 9 and then County Road 18 for approximately 10 miles. Turn right onto the road to Cape Crocker Park. You now have ahead of you 16 miles of winding back road, some of it gravel, and all of it unmarked. Numerous wrong turns are possible. Good luck—and take a county road map with you.

For *Lion's Head Lighthouse* from Highway 6 near the town of Ferndale, take County Road 9, also known as Lion's Head Road. Once in the town of Lion's Head, follow Main, Scott, and Helen streets to the lighthouse.

For *Cabot Head Lighthouse* from Highway 6, turn east onto Dyer's Bay Road approximately 2 miles north of Miller Lake and follow it for 8 miles. After passing through the village of Dyer's Bay, turn onto Cabot Head Road. The lighthouse is located at the end of the narrow, 5-mile-long access road.

THE IMPERIAL TOWERS

Cove Island Light – 1859

Nottawasaga Island Light – 1858

Chantry Island Light – 1859

Point Clark Light – 1859

To the east and south of the Bruce Peninsula and on islands just off the peninsula itself stand six magnificent stone sentinels. Their whitewashed limestone walls, in some cases more than five feet thick, soar up to ninety feet above the aquamarine waters of Lake Huron and Georgian Bay. Known collectively as the Imperial Towers, they are perhaps the most impressive and historic navigational markers in all of Canada.

Built during the 1850s, under Canadian rather than British authority, no one is sure today why they are called "Imperial." However, they are certainly imperial in the superlative sense of the word. Their elegant proportions and solid construction place them in a class entirely by themselves.

During the nineteenth century, lake sailors considered the Bruce Peninsula a death trap for ships, its wild and rugged shoreline threatening always to tear apart the hulls of wayward vessels. Recognizing the dangers that this knife-shaped peninsula posed to shipping, the Canadian government hired Ontario contractor John Brown to build a series of lighthouses marking prominent points and warning sailors away from ship-killing shoals.

A Scottish stonemason who had immigrated to Canada in the 1830s, Brown applied to the project his craftsman's zeal for quality and solid construction. If he was to do the job at all, he would do it right. But doing it right took far more time and money than the frugal Scotsman had ever imagined. As if angered by this

The Nottawasaga Lighthouse guards a small but treacherous island in Lake Huron's Georgian Bay.

human intrusion on its pristine shores, Lake Huron threw all its fury against Brown and his hardy work crews. Gales and blizzards repeatedly halted construction, storm-driven waves wrecked supply ships, and winter ice blocked access to building sites for months at a time. It took five long years to see the lantern in place atop the last of the six towers. By that time mishaps and cost overruns had eaten up all of Brown's profits, but he could point with pride to the Imperial Towers themselves, just as every Canadian citizen can do today.

Among the first of the tall towers built by John Brown and his hardy construction crew was the crucial Cove Island Lighthouse, which marks the Main Channel connecting Lake Huron to Georgian Bay. Work on the station apparently began as early as 1856 (the year is scratched into concrete inside the tower), and its light first guided sailors in 1858.

Since it stands on an island several miles from the mainland, visitors to the Bruce Peninsula likely won't see this light unless they take the ferry linking the tip of the peninsula to Manitoulin Island, a couple of dozen miles to the north. The two-hour ferry ride is a worthwhile adventure, however, and the lighthouse is spectacular —truly imperial. Against a lushly forested background, the whitewashed stone tower rises more than eighty-five feet above the lake. At the top, a red lantern room, encircled by a polygon of square windowpanes, houses a powerful, second-order Fresnel lens.

Well to the east of the Bruce Peninsula rises the sixty-foot tower of the Christian Island Lighthouse. Shortest of the Imperial Towers, the structure has stood the test of time. Completed during the late 1850s, it has never required substantial repairs. Several years ago, however, the lantern was removed and a

Passengers on ferries linking Manitoulin Island with the Bruce Peninsula often enjoy a spectacular view of Cove Island Lighthouse. An Imperial Tower, it soars more than eighty feet above Gig Point and the waters of Lake Huron. Completed in 1859, the station received a second-order Fresnel lens that is still operating.

Placed into service in 1859, the Chantry Island Lighthouse was automated almost a century later. Standing beside the tower is the roofless shell of its dwelling, destroyed by fire many years ago.

small, airport-style beacon fitted on a flat platform at the top. Without its lantern room the structure has the look of a medieval castle watchtower.

Vessels approaching Collingwood Harbor have often come to grief on the shoals and ledges that make the southern tip of Nottawasaga Bay a sailor's nightmare. To warn ships of the danger, Brown built the tallest of his towers here, on rugged Nottawasaga Island. The ninety-five-foot tower was ready for service in 1858. But the need for a light was so great that keepers hung a makeshift lantern from the unfinished tower each night until the work was complete and the official lighting apparatus in place. The light was automated in 1959, almost exactly 101 years after it went into service. It still does its job, but nowadays it does so without the help of a keeper.

Toward its southeastern end, the Bruce Peninsula is indented by a ten-mile-long rectangular slot known as Colpoy's Bay. Marking the southerly entrance to the bay is the fifty-five-foot-tall Imperial Tower on Griffith

Island. The tower dates to 1859 and, like the other Imperials, is a cylinder with thick walls of locally quarried limestone. Its light still guides vessels in and out of the bay and warns them away from the island.

Located on Chantry Island, near the far southwestern hip of the Bruce Peninsula, another of Brown's stone lighthouses still does the work it was built for in 1859. Warning ships away from the island and the rocky coastline beyond, the eighty-six-foot tower looks much like the other Imperials. Its light was automated in 1954.

About sixty miles south of the peninsula, the stubby thumb of Point Clark juts out into Lake Huron, pointing toward a shoal only two miles offshore. To warn ships of this dangerous obstacle, Brown's workmen built the last and, perhaps, the most spectacular of the Imperial Towers. Completed in 1859, the tower soars eighty-seven feet above the relatively flat headland. The Point Clark Lighthouse was declared a National Historic Site in 1967.

Now a National Historic Site, Point Clark Lighthouse may be the most spectacular of Canada's Imperial Towers.

HOW TO GET THERE:

Cove Island Lighthouse is best seen from the Manitoulin Island ferry. For ferry schedules and other information, call (519) 596–2510.

Christian Island and its decapitated lighthouse can be reached by ferry. As Highway 93 nears the town of Penetanguishene, turn north onto Highway 26 and follow it approximately 12 miles to the ferry dock. The route is winding, so keep a sharp eye out for signs.

Nottawasaga Island Lighthouse is not easily accessible from the mainland. It can be viewed from several points along the shore near the town of Collingwood, however, at the far southern tip of Nottawasaga Bay.

Located on an island off the southeastern edge of the Bruce Peninsula, the Griffith Island Lighthouse cannot be reached by road from the mainland. It is most easily seen from a boat or a small airplane.

Chantry Island Lighthouse can be viewed from Chantry Park in South Hampton. From Highway 21, turn toward Lake Huron onto High Street. Take a left onto Huron Street and then a right onto Beach Road.

Point Clark Lighthouse, the only Imperial Tower located on the mainland, is easy to reach by vehicle. From Highway 21 a few miles south of Kincardine, turn toward the lake onto Huron Concession 2 (a sign points the way to the lighthouse). After approximately 2.5 miles on HC2, turn left onto Huron Road and then right onto Lighthouse Road. The Canadian Parks Service maintains an excellent maritime museum in the keeper's dwelling. The museum is open from 10:00 A.M. to 5:00 P.M. during summer months.

A pair of lookalike dwarfs, the Wilson Channel Range Lighthouses mark the safe passage through a key channel separating St. Joseph's Island from the Ontario mainland. Built in 1905, they each stand about thirty feet tall. They serve as important navigational markers for ships traveling between the open waters of Lake Huron and the locks at Sault Ste. Marie.

BIBLIOGRAPHY

Adams, William Henry Davenport. *Lighthouses and Lightships: A Descriptive and Historical Account of Their Mode of Construction and Organization.* New York: Scribner's, 1870.

Adamson, Hans Christian. *Keepers of the Light.* New York: Greenberg, 1955.

Beaver, Patrick. *A History of Lighthouses.* Secaucus, N.J.: Citadel, 1972.

Bowen, Dana Thomas. *Shipwrecks of the Lakes.* Cleveland, Ohio: Freshwater Press, 1952.

Chase, Mary Ellen. *The Story of Lighthouses.* New York: Norton, 1965.

Havighurst, Walter. *The Great Lakes Reader.* New York: Macmillan, 1966.

Heming, Robert. *Ships Gone Missing: The Great Lakes Storm of 1913.* Chicago: Contemporary Books, 1992.

Holland, Francis Ross, Jr. *America's Lighthouses: Their Illustrated History Since 1716.* Brattleboro, Vt.: Stephen Greene Press, 1972.

———. *Great American Lighthouses.* Washington, D.C.: The Preservation Press, 1989.

Marx, Robert. *Shipwrecks of the Western Hemisphere.* New York: David McKay Company, 1971.

McCormick, William Henry. *The Modern Book of Lighthouses, Lifeboats, and Lightships.* London: W. Heinemann, 1913.

McKee, Russell. *Great Lakes Country.* New York: Crowell, 1966.

Moe, Christine. *Lighthouses and Lightships.* Monticello, Ill.: 1979.

Naush, John M. *Seamarks: Their History and Development.* London: Stanford Maritime, 1895.

Ratigan, William. *Great Lakes Shipwrecks and Survivals.* Grand Rapids, Mich.: Eerdmans Publishing, 1960.

Scheina, Robert L. "The Evolution of the Lighthouse Tower," *Lighthouses Then and Now* (supplement to the U.S. Coast Guard Commandant's Bulletin).

Snowe, Edward Rowe. *Famous Lighthouses of America.* New York: Dodd, Mead, 1955.

Tinney, James, and Mary Burdette-Watkins. *Seaway Trail Lighthouses: An Illustrated Guide.* Oswego, N.Y.: Seaway Trail, Inc., 1989.

United States Coast Guard. *Historically Famous Lighthouses.* CG-232, 1986.

LIGHTHOUSES INDEX

Numerals in italics indicate photograph/legend only.

Ashtabula Light, *34*

Barcelona Light, 31

Braddock Point Light, *9*

Buffalo Light Station, *24*

Buffalo Main Light, 28

Cabot Head Light, 74, 75–76

Cape Crocker Light, 74, 75–76

Chantry Island Light, 77, 79–80

Charlotte-Genesee Light, 17–18

Cheboygan Crib Light, *42*

Cleveland West Pierhead Light, 36

Cove Island Light, 77, 78, 80

DeTour Reef Light, *44*

Dunkirk Light, iv, 29–30

Erie Land Light, *33*

Fairport Harbor Light, 35

False Duck Island Light, 66–67

Fort Gratiot Light, 48

Fort Niagara Light, *3*, 20–21

Forty Mile Point Light, 54

Gibralter Point Light, 68–69

Goderich Main Light, *58*, 74, 76

Imperial Towers, 77–80

Janet Head Light, 71, 72

Kagawong Light, 71, 72–73

Kincardine Rear Range Light, 74–75, 76

Lights of Manitoulin Island, 71–73

Lights of the Bruce Peninsula, 74–76

Lights of Toronto, 68–69

Lightship *Huron*, 47

Lorain Light, 37–38

Marblehead Light, 39–40

Mississagi Straits Light, 71

New Presque Isle Light, 52–53

Nine Mile Point Light, 64–65

Nottawasaga Island Light, *60*, 77, 79, 80

Old Mackinac Point Light, 56

Old Presque Isle Light, 52–53

Oswego West Pierhead Light, 14

Poe Reef Light, *46*

Point Clark Light, 77, 79–80

Point Gratiot Light, 29–30

Pointe Aux Barques Light, 49

Point Burwell Light, 70

Presque Isle Light, 32

Prince Edward Point Light, *63*, 66–67

Queens Wharf Light, 69

Rock Island Light, 10

Round Island Light, *42*

Selkirk Light, 13

Sodus Point Light, 15

Sodus Point Pierhead Light, 6, *16*

South Baymouth Range Light, 71, 72–73

Spectacle Reef Light, *55*

Sturgeon Point Light, 51

Tawas Point Light, 50

Thirty Mile Point Light, 19

Tibbetts Point Light, v, 11–12

Toledo Harbor Light, 41

Vermilion Light, *22*

Wilson Channel Range Lights, *81*

FOR FURTHER INFORMATION
ON LIGHTHOUSES

Lighthouse Digest

P.O. Box 1690

Wells, ME 04090

(207) 646–0515

Lighthouse Digest publishes an interesting monthly devoted to lighthouse news.

U.S. Lighthouse Society

244 Kearny Street, 5th Floor

San Francisco, CA 94108

(415) 362–7255

Members receive an interesting quarterly magazine about lighthouses, and the society conducts worldwide tours of lighthouses.

Great Lakes Lighthouse Keepers Association

P.O. Box 580

Allen Park, MI 48101

The association publishes a quarterly journal for its members and hosts an annual meeting.

Lighthouse Preservation Society

P.O. Box 736

Rockport, MA 01966

The society is known as an advocacy group and sponsors lighthouse conferences.

U.S. Coast Guard

Historian's Office G-CP/H

2100 2nd Street, SW

Washington, DC 20593

The Coast Guard History Office maintains operational records and historical materials related to the U.S. Coast Guard and its predecessor agencies.

National Archives

Record Group 26

Washington, DC 20480

Record Group 26 constitutes records of the Bureau of Lighthouses and its predecessors, 1789–1939, as well as U.S. Coast Guard records, 1828–1947, and cartographic and audiovisual materials, 1855–1963. These records are at the main archives building in Washington, D.C. Some records, such as the individual lighthouse logs, are stored at the Suitland, Maryland, branch.

Ninth Coast Guard District

1240 East 9th Street

Cleveland, OH 44199–2060

The Ninth Coast Guard District is responsible for the operation and maintenance of the lighthouses on the Great Lakes. For permission to visit lighthouses not generally open to the public, contact the public affairs officer at this address.

The Great Lakes Historical Society

480 Main Street

Vermilion, OH 44089

(216) 967–3467

The Great Lakes Historical Society maintains an extensive museum and reference library on Great Lakes maritime history, including a wealth of information on lighthouses. It is well worth the time and effort to visit here.

Shore Village Museum

104 Limerock Street

Rockland, ME 04841

The Shore Village Museum has the most extensive collection of Fresnel lenses in America. A hands-on museum, it contains hundreds of lighthouse items.

National Park Service

Maritime Initiative

P.O. Box 37127

Washington, DC 20013-7127

(202) 343–9508

The Maritime Initiative is a database that contains the most accurate information available about American lighthouses.

PHOTO INFORMATION

The pictures for this book were taken on Fuji 50 and Fuji 100 slide film. I'm sure that other films would work just as well, but simplification is the only way I've survived as a professional travel photographer for the last few decades. I use only two Nikon Cameras (identical 8008s), with a small assortment of lenses. My tripod goes with me on every trip. When I was a young newspaper photographer, I thought that tripods were for sissy photographers who were afraid to blur images. Now I think that only fools don't use them. Then ensure sharp pictures even at slow shutter speeds and give you time to compose when looking into the finder. A small Nikon flash SP-24 which fits into my camera bag, completes the equipment, except for polarizing and warming filters.

The cover photo of Marblehead Lighthouse was taken on a Nikon 8008 camera with a 24-mm wide-angle lens at f 5.6 at 125th of a second with early evening, spring sunlight. A polarizing filter helped bring out the blue sky. The sailboat and the people just happened to be there.

When someone asks me how to take better lighthouse photos, I give them my 30-second "how to" suggestions.

First, try to arrive at the lighthouse when the light is interesting; sunrise or sunset are usually the two best times. Just before sunrise and just after sunset, there is wonderful, soft light on most days. Sometimes clouds at this time of day will reflect colors and help create mood; also the lighthouse beacon may be on and add interest. Other good times may be before an approaching storm or during fog. Unusual or "bad" weather may make good pictures.

Second, try using a telephoto lens. Because lighthouses are usually tall structures, there is a temptation to aim the camera up—and this creates the "falling-backward look," particularly when photographers use wide-angle lenses. Try backing away and using a telephoto to correct the distortion caused by a tilted camera. This also allows you to look for vantage points to shoot from that are often overlooked by other photographers.

For the picture of the Fresnel lens on page iv at Dunkirk, New York, I used the tripod and an exposure of eight seconds at f.8 on my 500-mm Nikon telephoto lens. I was standing on the ground about 200 feet from the tower; but, by using a telephoto lens, I was able to create the feeling of being right beside it. It was about forty-five minutes after sunset; later the sky would go black instead of the nighttime look of deep blue. I bracketed exposures—shooting one and two stops over and under as well as what I thought was the right setting. If it's worth shooting, I'm not stingy with film; besides, I see the film first when it comes back from processing and throw away the over and under stuff before anyone sees it. Editors think that I'm expert with exposures because they have never seen my wastebasket. [Now I know.—Ed.]

—Bruce Roberts

ABOUT THE AUTHORS

BRUCE ROBERTS and his wife, Cheryl, who helped with the research for this book, live on North Carolina's Outer Banks, not far from the Bodie Island Lighthouse. For many years Bruce was Senior Travel Photographer for *Southern Living* magazine. He started his career working as a photographer for newspapers in Tampa, Florida, and Charlotte, North Carolina. He is the recipient of many photography awards, and some of his photos are in the permanent collection of the Smithsonian Institution. Recently Bruce and Cheryl opened the Lighthouse Gallery & Gifts, a store devoted to lighthouse books, artifacts, and collectibles, in Nags Head.

RAY JONES is a freelance writer and publishing consultant living in Surry, a small town on the coast of Maine. He began his writing career working as a reporter for weekly newspapers in Texas. He has served as an editor for Time-Life Books, as founding editor of *Albuquerque Living* magazine, as a senior editor and writing coach at *Southern Living* magazine, and as founder and publisher of Country Roads Press. Ray grew up in Macon, Georgia, where he was inspired by the writing of Ernest Hemingway and William Faulkner, and worked his way through college as a disc jockey.